J. A Boyd

A summary of Canadian history

From the time of Cartier's discovery to the present day with questions adapted to each paragraph for the use of schools

J. A Boyd

A summary of Canadian history
From the time of Cartier's discovery to the present day with questions adapted to each paragraph for the use of schools

ISBN/EAN: 9783742843470

Manufactured in Europe, USA, Canada, Australia, Japa

Cover: Foto ©ninafisch / pixelio.de

Manufactured and distributed by brebook publishing software (www.brebook.com)

J. A Boyd

A summary of Canadian history

MANY histories of Canada have been written, but there is not one which, while comprehending in brief space the story of our three historic centuries, is not either confused and fragmentary in arrangement, or disfigured by gross blunders; while some are remarkable for a union of both defects. To supply a deficiency, therefore, the present little summary has been written. It aims at giving, in small compass, a full as well as accurate and connected relation of the chief incidents pertaining to Canadian History, from the time of Cartier's discovery to the present day. Many omissions have been supplied, many superfluities retrenched, many errors corrected, which deform popular text-books on this subject. The general arrangement adopted is that which has been naturally suggested by the progress of events. The questions appended to each chapter will be found available in the schoolroom. It is hoped that a book has thus been produced which will mainly serve for the instruction of Canadian youth in their country's history, and may be useful also as a manual of reference to all classes of readers.

TORONTO, *August*, 1860.

CONTENTS.

PART I.—CANADA UNDER THE FRENCH.

CHAPTER	PAGE
I.—From the Discovery of Canada to the Founding of Quebec,	7
II.—From the Founding of Quebec to the Death of Champlain,	15
III.—From the Death of Champlain to the Erection of Canada into a Royal Government,	23
IV.—From the Erection of Canada into a Royal Government to the Overthrow of French Dominion,	30

PART II.—CANADA UNDER THE BRITISH.

I.—From the Overthrow of French Dominion to the Division of the Province into Upper and Lower Canada,	57
II.—From the Division of the Province to its Re-union under one Government,	69
III.—From the Re-union of the Canadas to the Present Time,	111

SUMMARY

OF

CANADIAN HISTORY.

Part I.—CANADA UNDER THE FRENCH.

CHAPTER I.

FROM THE DISCOVERY OF CANADA TO THE FOUNDING OF QUEBEC.—EARLY VOYAGES.

I.—Our Continent was discovered by John and Sebastian Cabot, who, sailing from Bristol under the patronage of Henry VII. of England, landed on the Labrador coast in June, 1497, seventeen months before Columbus reached the mainland of tropical America. In 1524, Verrazzano, a Florentine navigator in the employment of Francis I. of France, sailed along the Atlantic seaboard from Florida to Cape Breton, and appropriated the whole in the name of his master under the title of "la Nouvelle France." Ten years after this, Captain Jacques Quartier, (or, more commonly, Cartier,) made his first voyage from St. Malo, in France, to the New World, and explored the north-eastern and western coasts of Newfoundland, (previously discovered by the Cabots.) He then proceeded to the mainland, entered the Miramichi river, sailed on to a large and picturesque bay, which was called "Golfe de Chaleur," by reason of the unwonted *heat* there experienced, and after running along the Gaspé coast, erected a cross bearing the inscription, " Vive le roy de France." Having thus taken possession of the country for Francis I., Cartier returned home.

DISCOVERY OF CANADA.

II.—Cartier, commissioned by the King, set out with three ships and 110 men on his second voyage, in May, 1535, when he was destined to discover Canada. His little fleet cast anchor in a small bay on the Labrador coast, on the 10th of August, and this day being dedicated to St. Lawrence, the voyagers styled their place of harbourage " la Baye St. Laurent." This name was afterwards transferred to the great river of Canada, and to the oceanic gulf into which it empties. Cartier next discovered the island of Anticosti, which he named " Assomption," and, sailing to the west, he entered the river St. Lawrence, which was greeted as the long-sought path to China and the East Indies. The wish to realize this single object dictated all the early voyages to America, and therefore, hopeful of success, Cartier pressed on till he reached the mouth of the Saguenay. Here he found several bands of Indians engaged in catching porpoises and other sea-fish, and was informed that the country of Canada lay beyond. Along the whole course of the river, the Commander discovered and named numerous islands, and among the rest, Isle aux Coudres, (from the abundance of *filberts* it produced,) and Isle de Bacchus, (from here having first seen grape-vines,) now called the Island of Orleans. Having reached this point, Cartier was visited on the 7th of September, by Donnacona, Lord of Canada, so-called, who received the French in a most friendly manner. The vessels were moored in the St. Charles, (then named " Sainte Croix,") in close proximity to the residence of Donnacona, which was in a village called Stadaconé, built upon the site of the lower town of Quebec. Many visits and presents were interchanged between the strangers and the natives, and at the request of the Chief, Cartier discharged 12 pieces of artillery, now first heard by the amazed Indians.

III.—The name Canada was understood and used by Cartier as applying simply to the country adjacent to Stadaconé, under the authority of Donnacona. But it is very probable that his use of the Indian term arose from a misapprehension of the savages' meaning. The Indians signified by this word any town, or village, or collection of huts, whereas Cartier supposed it to be said of the district. It is uncertain at what time "Canada" began to be used in its present extended sense.

IV.—Notwithstanding the endeavours of the Indians to prevent Cartier from penetrating farther into the country, he set forth (September 19) in two boats and a pinnace, bound for Hochelaga, a settlement higher up than the river. This place he reached after some danger and difficulty, (October 2,) and was hospitably entertained, according to custom, by the inhabitants. Hochelaga was a rudely-fortified Indian town, consisting of about fifty houses, sheltered by a beautiful mountain, which so delighted Cartier that he called it "Mont Royal," a name yet preserved in the corrupt form Montreal, assigned to the city at its base. After gaining some information respecting the country, he returned to his station at Sainte Croix, (October 11,) where he determined to winter. Unprepared to withstand the severity of the climate, and unprovided with proper food, scurvy broke out among his men, and cut off 26 of their number, before its ravages could be stopped. On May 3, Cartier erected a cross, 35 feet high, with a shield bearing the arms of France, and the words:—
"Franciscus primus, Dei gratia Francorum rex, reg-

nat." He seems to have doubted as to the friendliness of the natives; this suspicion, however, cannot exculpate him from the charge of treachery in seizing Donnacona and four of his Chiefs, and setting sail for France with the captives on board. This occurred three days after he had taken formal possession of his discoveries; the unfortunate Indians died soon after their arrival in Europe. After touching at the northern point of Cape Breton, and sailing along the southern coasts of Newfoundland (thus completing his circumnavigation of the island), Cartier arrived at St. Malo, on July 16, 1536.

VOYAGES OF CARTIER, ROBERVAL, AND DE LA ROCHE.

V.—The attention of the French King was awakened by Cartier's narration of his adventures, and by sundry interviews with the Indian Chiefs, and he nominated Jean François de la Rocque, Lord of Roberval, Viceroy in the countries of Canada, Hochelaga, and Saguenay, and Cartier was subordinated to him as Captain-General and Master-Pilot. Five ships were prepared at St. Malo, and as Roberval was unable to accompany Cartier at the time appointed, the latter, a third time in command, sailed forth, on May 24, 1541, to resume his explorations. Delayed by tempestuous weather, the expedition did not arrive at Ste. Croix till the end of August. Cartier told the Indians of Donnacona's death in France, and then moved a few leagues up the St. Lawrence to a more convenient harbour, now known as Cap-Rouge. Here he laid up three of his ships, and dispatched the others to France, to inquire respecting Roberval. He built a small fort in the vicinity of his ships, and another on the top of the overhanging cliff, and named the place Charlesbourg Royal. In the neighbourhood were found minerals resembling gold and silver, besides abundance of so-called diamonds, which afterwards gave name to the bold promontory, Cape Diamond. Cartier spent the autumn in exploring the river above Hochelaga, under the belief that a district said to be rich in minerals and precious stones, could be gained by this route. On the approach of winter, he returned to Fort Charlesbourg Royal. An attack was anticipated from the Indians, whose dislike for the French was daily increasing. Nevertheless, spring came without any bloodshed on either side, and Cartier, despairing of effecting any satisfactory result without Roberval, upon whom he depended for munitions and stores, resolved to return.

VI.—On his homeward voyage, he put into the harbour of St. John, Newfoundland, where he found Roberval with three vessels. These contained 200 souls, men, women, and children, thereby showing that it was the intention of the Governor to begin the colonization of the country. Roberval desired him to return, but for unexplained reasons, Cartier declined, and to prevent any dispute, the latter weighed anchor during the night, and continued his course. The discoverer of Canada died soon after his return to France; to his heirs was granted the exclusive privilege of Canadian trade for twelve years, which, however, was revoked four months after its bestowal.

VII.—Roberval, seemingly not discouraged by losing the experienced Cartier, prosecuted his voyage up the St. Lawrence as far as the commodious harbour of Cap-Rouge, where he disembarked. He repaired the partially-ruined forts which Cartier had thrown up eighteen months before, and occupied them during the winter. Justice was administered by him strictly: it is recorded that one Frenchman was hanged for committing theft, and that several were thrown into irons, or publicly whipped on account of other misdemeanours. The scurvy attacked his settlement, and about fifty died from its effects. In the spring, he set out with a select party to explore the Saguenay district, but after losing a boat and eight men, he was obliged to return. The same year he sailed back to France. Being engaged in the wars between Francis I. and Charles V., Roberval took no farther interest in Canada, until 1549, when he and his gallant brother, well-accompanied, embarked for the New World. But the whole expedition perished at sea, and every hope of an establishment in America was abandoned for nearly fifty years.

VIII.—Henry IV. having at length consolidated France, which had been rent asunder by civil and religious wars, gave to the Marquis de la Roche authority, as Lieutenant-General, to form a settlement in his transatlantic possessions. This nobleman accordingly gathered together a numerous body of settlers, partly drawn from French prisons, and embarked in 1598. Little is known of his proceedings save that before returning he landed fifty convicts to colonize Sable Island, a sterile sand-bank off the Nova Scotian coast. Seven years afterwards, twelve of these were found living, and being brought back to France, were pardoned and provided for by the King.

ESTABLISHMENT OF TRADING-POSTS.

IX.—The fur-trade of Canada had begun to attract attention in the commercial emporiums of France. Merchants of Dieppe, Rochelle, Rouen, and St. Malo, were gradually establishing temporary trading-posts, chiefly at Tadoussac, near the mouth of the Saguenay. Henry IV. regarded with favour the opening up of such communications, and in 1599, he entered into a contract with two distinguished traders, Pontgravé of St. Malo, and Chauvin of Rouen, whereby they engaged to transport and settle 500 emigrants in return for a monopoly of the St. Lawrence fur-trade. Captain Chauvin being appointed Lieutenant-General, made two voyages, brought out sixteen colonists, whom the kindness of the natives afterwards saved from starvation, and died in 1603, leaving, as his memorial, a house built of stone and mortar, the first erected in Canada, of which remains were lately to be seen at Tadoussac. His death put an end to the scheme.

X.—Commandeur de Chaste, Governor of Dieppe, was the third Lieutenant-General, and organized a company of merchants for the purposes of trade and discovery. He engaged the services of Samuel de Champlain, a bold and sagacious naval officer, who had gained a reputation in the West Indies, and with him was conjoined Pontgravé. These two were sent in command of an expedition to Tadoussac, and instructed, moreover, to ascend the St. Lawrence as far as possible. They accordingly passed Hochelaga, now dwindled into insignificance, but found themselves stopped by the Sault St. Louis, now known as the Lachine Rapids. Here landing, they made observations on the country and river. With these Champlain hastened to France, where he learned of De Chaste's death, and the derangement of the entire scheme. He explained, however, the results of his investigations to the King, who remained pleased with his diligence and success.

XI.—The conduct of the company, together with a monopoly of trade, was now transferred into the hands of Pierre du Guas, Sieur de Monts, whom the King appointed Lieutenant-General of New France, in 1603. De Monts and Champlain turned at first to Nova Scotia; they explored nearly all its coast-line, in 1606 and 1607, and were the founders of the colony of Acadia.

14 SUMMARY OF CANADIAN HISTORY.

Champlain then induced De Monts to direct his attention to Canada. Two vessels were accordingly fitted out and entrusted to Champlain and Pontgravé. The latter remained to foster the fur-trade at Tadoussac the former sailed past the island of Orleans, and selected a spot at the base of Cape Diamond, called by the natives Quebeio or Quebec, (meaning thereby a strait or narrow passage,) as suitable for the site of a town On the 3rd of July, 1608, Champlain laid the foundation of Quebec, the future capital of Canada. This was the earliest permanent settlement in America with the exception of Jamestown, in Virginia, which was founded in the previous year, 1607, by the English Captain Newport.

QUESTIONS TO CHAPTER I.

I. Who discovered America? In what year and under whose patronage was the discovery made? Where did Verrazzano sail? What title did he give to his discoveries? Who sailed after him? What discoveries did Cartier make?

II. When was Cartier's second voyage? What did he discover? Explain the reason of the name St. Lawrence? To what was it applied? What name was given to Anticosti? What was the object of the early voyages to America? Where did Cartier first meet the Indians? What Islands were named in the river? By whom was Cartier visited in September? Where did the Indian Chief live? What is now built on its site? Explain what passed between Cartier and the Indians.

III. In what sense was "Canada" used by Cartier? What did the Indians mean by the word?

IV. Where did Cartier next go? Describe Hochelaga. Explain the name Montreal. Where did Cartier winter? How was the winter passed? Describe the cross which was erected. Of what act of treachery was Cartier guilty?

What Island did he circumnavigate? When did he reach home?

V. How was the King's attention aroused? Who was the first Governor of Canada? To what posts was Cartier appointed How many voyages did Cartie make? How long did he occupy in the 3rd voyage? Where were the first forts built in Canada What was the place called? What were found in the neighbourhood? How was the autumn occupied? Why did Cartier resolve to return?

VI. Where did Cartier meet Roberval? How many people did Roberval bring with him? How did Cartier act? What was granted to Cartier's heirs?

VII. Where did Roberval disembark? What did he do on landing? Give instances of his severity. How many settlers did he lose, and in what manner When did he return to Canada What prevented him from returning before? What became of his second expedition? What effect had the loss upon France?

VIII. Who next received authority to form a settlement in Canada? From whom? Whence were his settlers partly drawn? When did he sail? Where did he land a colony, and with what result?

IX. What had begun to attract attention? Who established trading-posts? At what place? With whom, and when did the King enter into a contract? Explain the nature of their contract. What was Chauvin's success? What memorial did he leave?

X. Who organized a company of merchants? Whose services did he engage? Who commanded the expedition? How far did they ascend the St. Lawrence? What did Champlain learn on reaching France? What did he do notwithstanding?

XI. Who was placed at the head of the company? To what office was he appointed? Where did he first turn? When was Nova Scotia explored? Who founded the Colony of Acadia? To what place was attention next given? Who was sent out to Canada? Where did Pontgravé remain, and for what purpose? What was Champlain's object? When was Quebec founded? What was the first permanent settlement in America? By whom founded?

CHAPTER II.

FROM THE FOUNDING OF QUEBEC TO THE DEATH OF CHAMPLAIN.

ALLIANCE WITH THE HURONS AND ALGONQUINS.

I.—STADACONÉ, like Hochelaga, had dwindled away since the arrival of the French, and the few inhabitants who remained, lived in great part on the bounty of their European neighbours. In 1609, Champlain ascended the St. Lawrence and met a band of Algonquins, a large Indian tribe with whom he had formed an alliance at Stadaconé. Their territory stretched along the northern bank of the St. Lawrence, as far as the Ottawa, which was called the river of the Algonquins. The remainder of Canada to the west, was occupied chiefly by the Hurons, or Wyandots, who were extended from the Algonquin frontier to the great lake which now bears their name. Hochelaga was their chief village, as Stadaconé was that of the Algonquins. These two peoples were united and in constant hostility with the Iroquois, whose country lay to the south of the St. Lawrence, from Lake Erie to the Richelieu, which was known as the river of the Iroquois. This tribe was called by the English the Five Nations, being made up of the Onondagas, the Cayugas, the Senecas, the Mohawks, and the Oneidas, who formed one grand confederacy for offensive and defensive purposes. On the arrival of the French, a hereditary war was raging between the Huron-Algonquins and the Iroquois. It was necessary to take sides with one party or the other to escape the contempt of both; the French therefore chose those tribes nearest them, while as a natural consequence, the Iroquois allied themselves, in subsequent wars, to the English, with whose settlements they were conterminous. The Algonquins had guaranteed to Champlain a safe passage through the country, provided he agreed to assist them against the fierce and hostile Iroquois. They now called upon him to fulfil his promise, and Champlain, fetching a reinforcement from Tadoussac, accompanied them up the Richelieu, which opened into a spacious lake, now known as Lake Champlain, after the name of its celebrated explorer. A smaller sheet of water (now Lake George) was next entered, and here they came upon the barricaded encampment of Iroquois. The allies gained an easy victory, on account of the fire-arms of the French. On his return to Quebec, Champlain learned that De Monts' monopoly had been abrogated by the King, in compliance with the petitions of numerous French merchants, and this action involved his own return to France.

II.—De Monts managed to arrange with the traders of Rochelle and other cities, that in compensation for his affording them the use of the buildings at Quebec as a depot, they should assist him in all plans of settlement and discovery. He was thus enabled to dispatch Champlain to "Nouvelle France," as the country was now called, in 1610, with fresh supplies and reinforcements at his disposal. After a remarkably rapid passage of eighteen days, Champlain reached Tadoussac. On arriving at Quebec he again complied with the invitation of the Algonquins, and joined in an attack upon the Iroquois, in which the latter were defeated. He shortly afterwards left for France, on hearing of Henry IV.'s assassination, but returned in 1611, to fix upon the place for a new settlement higher up the river than Quebec. This resulted in the choice of a spot adjoining Cartier's Mont Royal, which he cleared, sowed, and enclosed by means of an earthen wall.

III.—The colony at Quebec was flourishing exceedingly; the cultivation of the soil had been successful; the labours of the settlers had been unmolested; peace and prosperity satisfied the wishes of all. Champlain now formed plans with his Algonquin friends for more extensive schemes in the way of discovery and colonization, and therefore returned to France to furnish himself with the necessary resources. De Monts had resigned his appointment, and was succeeded by Count de Soissons, as Viceroy of the country. The latter entered into the plans of Champlain, whom he constituted his Lieutenant, with the right to exercise all those functions which pertained to himself. But very soon after, the Count died, and the Prince of Condé was created Viceroy (1612). He in like manner became the warm supporter of the enterprising Champlain, and delegated to him the same powers as those conferred by his former patron.

CHAMPLAIN, GOVERNOR OF CANADA, 1612.

IV.—Champlain, as Deputy-Governor, and with the delegated authority of Viceroy, sailed for the colony in March, 1613, accompanied by several French merchants. In a previous expedition, Champlain had named that part of the river above the St. Louis rapids, La Chine, believing it to lead to China; he was now induced by the story of a deceitful Frenchman, who had lived among the Indians, to undertake a laborious journey up the Ottawa, nearly as far as Lake Nipissing, under the impression that he would thus reach the North Sea, and discover a North-west passage to the East Indies. Having been undeceived by the Indians, he returned by the same route, and sailed for France to further the interests of the colony. He found no difficulty in equipping another expedition from Rouen and St. Malo, which came to Quebec in 1615. This had been joined by four fathers of the Récollet order, who were the first priests in Canada. Champlain now engaged in a long tour with his Indian allies,—up the Ottawa to Lake Nipissing, and thence to Lake Huron. They next turned to the South, and reached the shores of Lake Ontario, (then first discovered,) and subsequently, crossing the St. Lawrence, came upon the main object of their expedition: an Iroquois settlement defended by palisades, which they prepared to storm. Champlain, however, was twice wounded in the leg, and the allies were forced to retreat. The Governor occupied the winter in exploring, and did not reach Tadoussac till the spring of the following year, whereupon he sailed for Honfleur, in September, 1616.

V.—He found the Prince of Condé disgraced and imprisoned, in consequence of his share in the disturbances during the minority of Louis XIII. After much controversy, it was settled that the Duke of Montmorency, Lord High Admiral, should purchase Condé's office of Viceroy for 11,000 crowns. The associated merchant company, formed in 1610, was prevented from embarking in further operations by disputes between Rochelle and the other cities. Attempts were also made, but in vain, to degrade Champlain from his high position. At length everything was quieted, and Champlain with his family sailed in 1620, for the land of his adoption. He learned on arriving, that an Indian conspiracy against the French settlers had been suppressed by one of the missionaries. The total number of the colonists, notwithstanding all his exertions, amounted to no more than sixty. He found that the various settlements had been neglected, and proceeded to strengthen that at the Three Rivers, by erecting a fort. He was disheartened also by the information, that certain adventurers from Rochelle, in violation of the company's privileges, had bartered for furs with the Indians, heedlessly giving them fire-arms in exchange. The Récollets were now busied in erecting their first convent on the banks of the St. Charles near Quebec. The first child of French parents was born in Quebec, in 1621. The same year, most unexpected intelligence reached Champlain. Montmorency had deprived the merchants' association of their privileges, and had transferred all colonial trade to the Sieurs de Caen, uncle and nephew, of whom the latter was coming to assume its personal superintendence. Champlain was thus superseded and subjected to the control of another. In July, De Caen arrived at Tadoussac, and acted in the most harsh and arbitrary manner, seizing the vessels belonging to the merchants, and disregarding Champlain's remonstrances. His violent measures reduced the colony to forty-eight, the rest returning to France, whither De Caen soon followed. Champlain now managed to effect a temporary treaty of peace between the continually-warring Indians. After this he busied himself in erecting a stone fort named St. Louis, at Quebec, and on its completion he departed to France in search of farther aid.

VI.—Meanwhile, in the mother country, a sort of union had been formed between the old company and the De Caens, but with so little cordiality on either side, that Montmorency was glad to relieve himself from trouble, by disposing of his viceroyalty to the Duke de Ventadour. The sole object of this energetic religionist was to diffuse the Roman Catholic faith in the New World. In 1625, he added three Jesuits and two lay brothers to the Récollets already in Canada, and laid illiberal restrictions upon Protestant worship. Dissensions were now breaking forth again between the Iroquois and the Algonquins; Champlain exerted himself to the utmost to avert the threatened hostilities, but in vain, and war recommenced with barbaric fury.

VII.—The De Caens were Huguenots, and, withal, more interested in profiting by the fur-trade than in developing the resources of the country. Cardinal Richelieu therefore superseded their consolidated company by another, known as the Company of One Hundred Associates, to which a charter was granted in 1627. This company undertook to send out a large body of settlers, and to provide them with all requisites for three years, after which time land, with enough corn for seed, was to be given them; the colonists were to be Roman Catholic Frenchmen; and, moreover, to each settlement, three priests were to be allotted, who should be cared for during fifteen years, after which, glebes were to be assigned to them sufficient for their support. In return, the King made over to the company the fort and settlement at Quebec, and all New France, with power to appoint judges, confer titles, and generally to administer the Government. It received a monopoly of the fur-trade and other branches of commerce, the cod- and whale-fisheries excepted, which were reserved for the benefit of all subjects. The viceroyalty was now suspended, and Champlain was appointed Governor of the colony.

VIII.—Richelieu's famous scheme was interrupted by the breaking out of a war between France and England. Sir David Kertk, (Anglicé Kirk,) a French Calvinist refugee in the British service, was commissioned in 1628, by Charles I., to conquer Canada. He intercepted some of the company's ships, burned the village at Tadoussac, and then summoned Quebec to surrender. Champlain refused, and Kirk retreated for the time being. In 1629 his brothers Louis and Thomas Kirk, with a squadron of three ships, sent by him, appeared before Quebec, in which place both provisions and ammunition were well-nigh exhausted. On their proffer of honourable conditions, Champlain felt himself justified in surrendering Quebec and all Canada into the hands of the English. The settlers (at this time not much outnumbering one hundred souls) who wished to remain were allowed so to do; those who preferred to go were permitted to retain arms, clothes, and baggage, and were provided with a passage to France. Champlain hastened home, and so influenced the cabinet of Louis XIII. that the restoration of Canada was stipulated for in the articles of peace which were being negotiated between the two powers. The peace of St. Germain-en-Laye was signed on 29th March, 1632, whereby New France was handed back to the mother country.

IX.—It will not be deemed extraordinary that both England and France regarded with indifference the loss or acquisition of Canada at this time, since the only settlements were comprised in a fort, barracks, and some houses at Quebec, with a few fishing- and trading-huts at Tadoussac, Montreal, and Three Rivers. The year of the peace, two Jesuits came in a ship of their own to the work of evangelizing Canada, of whom Paul le Jeune has been styled "the father of Jesuit missions." Richelieu's company was now re-invested with its privileges, and Champlain again appointed to his former office as Governor. In 1633, a fleet was prepared, which carried out more property than at that time existed in the colony. Prosperity was in some measure checked by restrictions laid upon professors of the reformed religion, ever the most enterprising colonizers; while Roman Catholicism was more firmly established by the erection of religious and educational institutions, under the control of the Jesuits. Schools for children were opened in Quebec, by Father Lalemant. A son of the Marquis de Gamache, Réné de Rohault, who had joined the Jesuits, founded a college at Quebec for the education of youth, and also an Indian school, towards the close of 1635.

X.—On December 25, 1635, Champlain died at Quebec. His remains were interred in the settlement he had founded. His name stands in the annals of our country, equally illustrious with that of the discoverer, Cartier, as the one man who gave success and permanence to French colonization. He identified himself with the progress of Canada for nearly thirty years, and by his untiring energy and perseverance, overcame the apathy of French courtiers and French merchants, more eager to enrich themselves than to disseminate the blessings of civilization and Christianity.

QUESTIONS TO CHAPTER II.

I. What places had dwindled away since the arrival of the French? What did Champlain do in 1609? Name the principal Indian tribes in Canada. Where was the Algonquin country situated? Name their river. Give the limits of the Hurons. Name the chief villages of both. What nations were always at war? Give the Iroquois boundaries. What did the English call this nation, and why? With what party did the French side? What was the arrangement between Champlain and the Algonquins? Where did he accompany them? For what purpose? What did Champlain learn on his return?

II. What arrangement did De

Monts make? What was Canada now called? What was the length of his passage in 1610? What did he do on arriving? Where was the place for a new settlement chosen? In what year?

III. What was the condition of things at Quebec? What plans did Champlain now form? Who succeeded De Monts? Who followed him? How did Condé act towards Champlain?

IV. In what capacity did Champlain return? What name was given to the river above the St. Louis rapids? Why so called? What journey did Champlain undertake, and why? When and where was another expedition equipped for Canada? Who came in this expedition? Describe Champlain's tour, and the results of it. When did he return to France?

V. In what position did Champlain find the Prince of Condé? Who succeeded the Prince? What company had been formed in 1610? How was it now prevented from acting? When and with whom did Champlain return to Canada? What did he learn on arriving? What was the number of the colonists? Where was a fort erected? What disheartened him? When was the first child born in Canada, and where? How was Champlain temporarily suspended? In what manner did Champlain now occupy himself? To what number did De Caen reduce the colony?

VI. Why and to whom did Montmorency dispose of his office? What was his successor's object, and in what way did he further it? What dissensions were breaking forth in Canada?

VII. Why did Richelieu supersede the De Caens' company? What was the new company called, and when was it chartered? What did the company undertake to do? What return did the King make? What change was made in the Government?

VIII. What interrupted Richelieu's scheme? Who was sent against Quebec? With what result in 1628? What happened in 1629? What conditions were granted to the settlers? What was Champlain's action? When and where was peace signed?

IX. Why was the gain or loss of Canada regarded with indifference? Who was the father of Jesuit missions, and when did he arrive in Canada? What is said of the company and Champlain? How was prosperity checked? How was Roman Catholicism more firmly established? Who opened schools for children? When and by whom was the Jesuit College founded at Quebec? What school was established?

X. When did Champlain die? Where was he buried? What eulogy may be passed upon him?

CHAPTER III.

FROM THE DEATH OF CHAMPLAIN TO THE ERECTION OF CANADA INTO A ROYAL GOVERNMENT.

CHARLES HUALT DE MONTMAGNY, GOVERNOR, 1636.

I.—AFTER Champlain's death, a temporary Governor was appointed in the Commandant at Three Rivers, M. de Chasteaufort who was succeeded in 1636, by Charles de Montmagny. Trade was now languishing, and the company had become indifferent to the success of the colony. But great vigour was manifested in religious concerns. Under the auspices of the Duchess d'Aiguillon, a party of Ursuline Nuns founded the Hôtel-Dieu, at Quebec, in 1639. Madame de la Peltrie brought out at her own charge, another body of Nuns, who established the Ursuline Convent. The Abbé Olivier, who had originated the order of St. Sulpice, projected a plan for founding a Seminary in Canada. The importance of Montreal marked it out as a suitable locality, and in 1640, the entire island was ceded by the King to a company of about fifty persons of eminence. In 1664, this company handed over the island and seigneury of Montreal to the order of St. Sulpice. In 1642, Montreal (called at first Ville-Marie) was founded by M. de Maisonneuve, who, in command of a party from France, erected the first fort, whilst the superior of the Jesuits consecrated the site. In the following year, two ladies of fortune founded the Hôtel-Dieu at Montreal.

II.—The Iroquois after Champlain's death renewed their attacks upon the Algonquins and the Hurons. They had conquered the former nation, had nearly subdued the Hurons, and were now menacing the French. The Governor therefore erected and garrisoned a fort at the mouth of the Richelieu, by which river they usually descended, in order to check their advance; whereupon the Iroquois, awed by this measure, concluded peace with him and his Indian allies. This, however, lasted but for a short time.

LOUIS D'AILLEBOUST DE COULONGE, GOVERNOR, 1648.

Montmagny was removed from office in consequence of the King's decree, that no colonial Governor should hold office for a longer term than three years, and was succeeded by M. d'Ailleboust in 1648, who had previously been Commandant at Three Rivers. A few years later Margaret Bourgeois founded a seminary at Montreal, known as the Daughters of the Congregation.

III.—The Jesuit Missionaries had been continually preaching among the Indians, and finding the Hurons most tractable, had baptized several thousands of them. These converts were then induced to unite in villages. St. Joseph on Lake Huron, was the village where an Indian congregation first met for Christian worship. In 1648, the Iroquois seemed resolved to exterminate the Hurons, and suddenly fell upon their unsuspecting villages. St. Joseph was singled out for attack, and whilst the priest Daniel was performing service, a band of Iroquois burst upon the unarmed inhabitants, massacred every one of them to the extent of 400 families, and last of all put the good father to a martyr's death.

At this time the first communication passed between the French and British American colonies. An envoy from New England brought proposals for a lasting peace and alliance with Canada, despite all hostilities of the mother countries,—a proposition which M. d'Ailleboust announced himself by a deputy at Boston as willing to entertain, provided that the English united with him against the Iroquois. This proviso was not acceptable to the Puritans, and the negotiation ended.

Again did the Iroquois descend upon the Huron settlements: St. Ignace and St. Louis were desolated and given to the flames, and the Jesuit missionaries killed; shortly after St. Johns, with nearly 8000 inhabitants, was totally destroyed. The decimated Hurons now abandoned themselves to despair, and fled in all directions. Some took refuge among the Eries and Ottawas and other more remote Nations, and some united with their Iroquois conquerors; some, under the direction of the Jesuits, removed to the island of St. Joseph, where their inveterate foes soon found them out and well-nigh annihilated them. An unhappy remnant of some hundreds sought aid from the missionaries, and was by them conveyed to a post near Quebec. The descendants of these refugees are still to be found in the village of Lorette, a few miles from Quebec. At this juncture the French were virtually blockaded in their forts, and the Iroquois remained masters of the country. About this time the traders at Tadoussac introduced intoxicating liquors among the tribes of the Saguenay, and drunkenness became so frequent and so injurious that the chiefs petitioned the governor to imprison all natives found guilty of this offence.

JEAN DE LAUSON, GOVERNOR, 1651.

IV.—In 1651, M. d'Ailleboust was replaced by M. de Lauson, one of the principals of Richelieu's company. Colonial affairs were not very promising; the Iroquois were increasing in audacity and harassing the French at all points. So dangerously beset was the island of Montreal that M. de Maisonneuve, the local governor, went in search of succour to France, whence he returned in 1653 with a reinforcement of 105 men. In consequence of this and in part through the self-denying labour of missionaries, the Iroquois sued for peace, which it was thought prudent to grant. In 1655, the Onondagas solicited that a French settlement should be made in their country, which De Lauson after some hesitation complied with. Sieur Dupuis and 50 men, together with 4 missionaries, were accordingly appointed to form this station, and to found the first Iroquois church. This movement excited the jealousy and suspicions of the other four Iroquois tribes, and 400 Mohawks in consequence attempted to intercept the party of French; they only succeeded, however, in pillaging a few canoes. The same band of marauders attacked a body of christianized Hurons, working on the island of Orleans, and carried them off into bondage without any attempt at rescue on the part of the governor. At length Iroquois insolence became insupportable, and the French determined on war. Dupuis and his little colony, meanwhile, managed to escape with great address from their critical position, and reached Montreal safely in fifteen days.

PIERRE DE VOYER, VISCOUNT D'ARGENSON, GOVERNOR, 1658.

V.—A succession of changes now took place in the government: de Lauson was succeeded by his son, who in turn gave way to the former governor D'Aillehoust, who was superseded in 1658 by Viscount d'Argenson. The very day after he landed, the Iroquois massacred some Algonquins under the very guns of Quebec, and escaped from the 200 French that were sent in pursuit. The same year the Mohawks met with a severe check in an attempt to surprise Three Rivers. In 1659, the indefatigable François de Laval, Abbé de Montigny, arrived at Quebec to preside over the Roman Catholic Church as apostolic vicar. On the erection of Quebec into an episcopal see, fifteen years later, Laval became the first bishop.

PIERRE DU BOIS, BARON D'AVAUGOUR, GOVERNOR, 1661.

VI.—In 1661, Argenson was relieved by Baron d'Avaugour, who by his representations to the King seems to have saved Canada from abandonment by the colonists. He pictured to Louis XIV. the helpless state

of the country, and induced him to send M. de Monts
to investigate the state of affairs ; 400 troops, moreover, were added to the colonial garrison. The govern-
or having permitted the sale of ardent spirits, in spite
of the protestations of the clergy, disorder arose to a
deplorable height. Laval hastened to France, and by
his remonstrances succeeded in obtaining such powers
as were necessary to check the fatal commerce. On his
return he founded and endowed the Quebec Seminary
in 1663 (now Laval University). In the same year, a
remarkable series of violent earthquakes, recurring two
or three times a day, and continuing with slight inter-
mission for half-a-year, agitated the entire surface of
Canada; it is singular to learn that no loss of life or
permanent injury was occasioned by these repeated
shocks.

VII.—An attempt at peace on the part of the Iroquois was frustrated by an ambuscade of the Algonquins, who intercepted and killed the deputation. The
Iroquois had about this time procured fire-arms from
the Dutch at Manhattan, (they first received them from
the Dutch on the Ohio in 1640,) and thus acquired an
incontestable superiority over all the other aborigines.
They now attacked those tribes who had given refuge
to the Hurons, and commenced by driving the Ottawas
into the islands of Lake Huron. They next engaged in
a desperate struggle with the Eries, who were finally
exterminated, leaving no memorial of their existence
except in the lake that bears their name.

VIII.—Baron d'Avaugour was now recalled, partly on account of the liquor-traffic, partly on account of complaints against his stern administration.
Louis XIV., influenced, it is said, by Laval, and second-
ed by his able minister Colbert, resolved to rescue Canada from misgovernment, and to render every assist-

ance necessary for the well-being of the colonists, at this time numbering 2000. The Associated Company resigned all their rights into the hands of the King, who transferred the same, with like conditions, to the West India Company, whose powers were yet kept in abeyance for some time. Heretofore all civil and military authority had been vested in the governor. The executive function was now separated from the legislative. Canada was transformed into a royal government, with a Council of state nominated by the Crown to co-operate with the Governor in the administration of affairs. This sovereign Council was to consist of the Governor, the Bishop, the Intendant, and five (afterwards twelve) leading residents. Courts of law were established at Quebec, Montreal, and Three Rivers, and the laws of France, the "Coutûme de Paris," became the legal code. An Intendant was appointed, who combined the duties of Minister of Justice, of Finance, of Police, and of Public Works. Grants of land continued to be made, in the form of Seigneuries, by royal edict. Questions of feudal law were subject to the decree of the Governor and the Intendant.

QUESTIONS TO CHAPTER III.

I. Who succeeded Champlain? What religious institutions were established? Who thought of founding a Seminary in Canada? What was the site selected, and when ceded? By whom and when was Montreal founded? To whom was Montreal given in 1664?

II. What was the condition of Hurons and Algonquins? Why was a fort erected at the mouth of the Richelieu? What effect had it? Why was Montmagny removed? Who succeeded him, and in what year? What did Margaret Bourgeois found, and where?

III. What was the effect of Jesuit preaching among the Indians? What distinguished the village of St. Joseph? What did the Iroquois resolve on in 1648? Describe the attack upon St. Joseph. At what time did communication pass between the British and French colonists? What was the purport of it, and how did it end? Describe the second attack of the Iroquois. What was its effect upon the Hurons? Where is a remnant of the Hurons to be found at present? What was the relative position of the French and Iroquois? What commerce had been introduced at Tadoussac, and with what result?

IV. Who and what was the

next Governor? Why did the Governor of Montreal repair to France, and with what result? What induced the Iroquois to sue for peace? What did the Onondagas desire? How did the Governor act? What was the effect among the other Iroquois tribes? Describe the conduct of the Mohawks. What became of Dupuis' colony?

V. Mention the official changes which took place in the government. Give the occurrences of 1658. Who was first Apostolic Vicar in Canada, and when did he arrive? To what place and in what year was the first bishop appointed in Canada?

VI. Who succeeded Argenson? What did he do for the country? What induced Laval to go to France? What institution was founded in 1663, and by whom? What occurred in the same year?

VII. What frustrated peace with the Iroquois? From whom and when did the Iroquois first receive fire-arms? What was the subsequent effect of this acquisition? and exemplify.

VIII. Why was Avaugour recalled? Who co-operated with Louis XIV. in his Canadian schemes? What was now the number of the colonists? What company succeeded the "100 Associates"? Describe the constitutional changes made in the government. What were the Intendant's functions? How were grants of land made and questions of feudal law decided?

CHAPTER IV.

FROM THE ERECTION OF CANADA INTO A ROYAL GOVERNMENT TO THE OVERTHROW OF FRENCH DOMINION IN CANADA.

AUGUSTIN DE SAFFRAY-MÉSY, GOVERNOR, 1663.

I.—Augustin de Mésy, appointed in 1663, was the first Governor under the new régime. He was a man of haughty and obstinate temper, and having quarrelled with his Council, he took upon himself to send back to France two of its principal members,—an arbitrary act which procured his own recall. He died at Quebec, however, before the dispatch arrived.

ALEXR. DE PROUVILLE, MARQUIS DE TRACY, VICEROY, 1665.

The Marquis de Tracy arrived in Quebec in 1665, as Viceroy and Lieutenant-General; De Courcelles was named under him as Governor, and Jean Talon as Intendant. The Viceroy brought with him the whole regiment of Carignan, who had acquired renown in Hungary against the Turks. With these came likewise a large body of settlers, bringing sheep, cattle, and horses, (now first introduced into Canada,) so that the colony in a few years of immigration received an accession of numbers exceeding its former population. Prompt measures were taken against the Iroquois, and three forts were erected on the Richelieu so as to cover the French settlements: one at Sorel, one at Chambly, and the third nine miles higher up the river. Three of the Nations speedily came to terms, but the Mohawks and Oneidas kept aloof sullenly. De Courcelles first took the field against them, and afterwards the Marquis in person, but the Indians never risked an encounter, and the French, after traversing about 700 miles of country, were obliged to content themselves with burning the various villages they passed through. Most of the officers belonging to the Carignan regiment settled in the country and received grants of land with Seigneurial tenure from the King. Having placed the Colony in a state of defence and established the authority of the West India Company, the Viceroy returned home in 1667, leaving De Courcelles at the head of the Government, and ruling over a population of 4312. Before his departure, a peace was concluded with the Indians, in 1666, which lasted for eighteen years. This nobleman's term of office is further memorable, from the fact that trade-monopoly, so fatal to all colonial enterprise, was abolished during his administration, chiefly at Talon's instance, (with certain exceptions in favour of the West India Company,) so that the colonists were permitted freedom of trade with the Indians, and the mother country.

DANIEL DE REMY DE COURCELLES, GOVERNOR, 1667.

II.—This Governor by skilful diplomacy sverted a threatened Indian war, and in the interval of peace the enterprising Intendant, M. Talon, dispatched Nicholas Perrot to visit the distant western and northern tribes. This bold traveller penetrated 1200 miles into the wilderness, as far as the great lakes, and induced Indian deputies from all the neighbouring Nations to assemble at the Falls of St. Mary, between Lakes Superior and Huron. There the assembled chiefs were met, in 1671, by Sieur de St. Lusson, who persuaded them to acknowledge the sovereignty of his King, and erected a cross with the arms of France.

The Governor had fixed upon Cataraqui, on Lake Ontario, near the present site of Kingston, as an eligible point for the erection of a fort, his object being to protect the fur-traders, and to check Indian incursions. He visited the spot in person, but was so much injured in health by exposure and hardship, that on his return to Quebec he desired to be relieved from the burden of office. About 1670, the small-pox broke out with the utmost violence among the Indians, and many tribes were all but exterminated by its terrible ravages.

LOUIS DE BUADE, COUNT DE PALUAN AND DE FRONTENAC GOVERNOR, 1672.

III.—The Count de Frontenac assumed the government in 1672. He caused the fort at Cataraqui to be built immediately, and gave it his own name, Frontenac —a name still applied to the county in which Kingston is situated. In 1674, the West India Company was suppressed by Louis XIV.

During Frontenac's administration, an extensive scheme of exploration was planned by the Intendant, Talon. News had reached him from the Far West respecting a vast river which flowed in a southerly direction. He entrusted to Father Marquette and an adventurous merchant of Quebec, named Joliet, the dangerous task of ascertaining the truth of this report. They set out with two canoes and six men, and after many adventures these explorers discovered the mighty Mississippi, and sailed down its stream past the mouths of the Missouri, Ohio, and Arkansas. At this point they turned and commenced a homeward journey. Marquette remained among the friendly Miamis, at the extremity of Lake Michigan, and Joliet alone reached Quebec, where he found that Talon had departed for France. A young Frenchman, named La Salle, was fired with Joliet's narrative, and in the hope of being able to reach China in this way, he departed to France to organize an expedition. Being joined by the Chevalier de Tonti and under the patronage of the Prince of Conti, he embarked for Quebec with thirty men, in 1678. He had received from the King the Seigneury of Cataraqui, and after his arrival, rebuilt Fort Frontenac of solid stone. Accompanied by Father Hennepin, who was the historian of the voyage, La Salle's party hastened on to the West. Above the Niagara Falls, La Salle constructed a vessel of 60 tons and carrying 7 guns, which he called the "Griffon;" this was the first vessel built on Canadian waters. In this he sailed to Lake Michigan, where he established a trading post, as he had previously done at Niagara and Detroit. The Griffon was sent back, laden with rich furs, and bound for Niagara, but never being heard of subsequently, it is believed she foundered in a storm. La Salle, meanwhile, was pressing on undauntedly, and having embarked on the Mississippi, he followed the windings of that river to its outlet in the Gulf of Mexico. He took possession of all the country along its banks in the name of his master Louis XIV., from whom it was styled Louisiana, and after an absence of more than two years he regained Quebec.

IV.—Frontenac, though talented and energetic, was self-willed, suspicious, and domineering, and as may be thought, he was engaged in continual disputes, of which the chief were with Laval and the clergy on account of the liquor-traffic, and again with Duchesneau, the Intendant who had replaced the illustrious Talon. The home government in consequence decided on recalling him, and likewise the Intendant.

LE FEBVRE DE LA BARRE, GOVERNOR, 1682.

In 1682, M. de la Barre arrived as Governor, and M. de Meules as Intendant. At this time the French population of Canada was about 10,000 souls. War was now threatening to recommence between the French and the Iroquois. Since New York had passed into the hands of the English, these Indians found it more for their profit to leave the French traders and to carry their peltries to an English market. They even bought up the furs of all Indians in alliance with the French for the same purpose. Grievous complaints were made by the Canadian Colony, but the Iroquois, being assured of British support, entirely disregarded them. This astute race soon began to perceive the means of giving influence to their own position, by remaining as far as possible neutral, in the rivalry which was now becoming manifest between the two bodies of European colonists. This state of affairs was reported on by a general assembly convoked by the Governor, and a memorial was transmitted to Paris. At length La Barre, on the arrival of a detachment of 200 soldiers from France, was prepared to administer chastisement to the perverse Iroquois. He marched up the river to Lake Ontario, where was appointed a place of meeting between him and the Indian deputies. Notwithstanding his high resolves, he found his army, on arriving at the place, so reduced by sickness and want of food, that he was obliged to accede to the demands of the deputies, withdraw his army, and retreat to Quebec. Here he found to his mortification that a fresh reinforcement of troops had arrived, bearing despatches from the King, relative to the conduct of a triumphant war against the Five Nations.

JACQUES RENÉ DE BRISAY, MARQUIS DE DENONVILLE, GOVERNOR, 1685.

V.—In consequence of dissatisfaction felt at his want of success, La Barre was replaced, in 1685, by the Marquis de Denonville, who had been specially selected on account of his distinguished valour. He saw the necessity for thoroughly humbling the haughty savages, and laid plans for building a fort at Niagara, to intercept the communications of the British with the Iroquois. In 1686, he received a warning letter from the Governor of New York, informing him that the Iroquois were the subjects of England, and therefore under that kingdom's protection. In the following year, a large reinforcement of 800 men, under the Chevalier de Vaudreuil, arrived from France, whereupon the Governor dishonourably seized a number of Iroquois chiefs, whom he had plausibly induced to assemble at Fort Frontenac, and forwarded them to France to labour in the King's galleys. After a skirmish in which the Iroquois were repulsed, the Governor erected a fort at Niagara, and garrisoned it with 100 men. A fatal disease shortly after cut off nearly all the garrison, and the survivors abandoned the post, which the Indians soon destroyed. The French fort at Chambly, on the Richelieu, was attacked by the Iroquois, apparently instigated by their English neighbours. The assailants, however, were repulsed, though they devastated the surrounding settlement. Fort Frontenac was with difficulty sustained against the same indefatigable foes, who blockaded it at all points. Strange to relate, the Iroquois at this juncture proffered peace, which the Governor accepted with humiliating conditions. Some of the Hurons, however, who wished the utter destruction of their hereditary enemies, managed by sundry acts of dissimulation and treachery, to break up the newly-formed peace. 1400 Iroquois instantly laid waste the island of Montreal, slaughtered all who opposed them, and carried off 200 prisoners (1689). The French were filled with consternation, blew up Fort Frontenac, burned two vessels, and abandoned the Western Lakes. At this crisis, French Canada was virtually reduced to the forts at Montreal, Three Rivers, and Quebec, with the post at Tadoussac.

LOUIS DE BUADE, COUNT DE PALUAN AND DE FRONTENAC, GOVERNOR FOR THE SECOND TIME, 1689.

VI.—When affairs were at this extremity, the government was entrusted for the second time to the experienced hands of the Count de Frontenac, who returned to Canada in 1689, and brought with him the Iroquois chiefs whom his predecessor had so basely entrapped. By restoring these captives, the Indians were for a time pacified; but the Ottawas and other allies of the French began to make overtures to the Iroquois, in order to enjoy a share in the English trade. The Governor thought it now a prudent stroke of policy, to prevent this union, by showing to the natives that the French were superior in power and resources to their rivals, the English. There was at this time war between the two monarchies, in consequence of the Revolution of 1688, when Louis XIV. espoused the cause of the outcast James II. The Count de Frontenac therefore organized three expeditions to invade the British settlements. The first marched from Montreal in 1690, surprised Corlaer or Schenectady, the frontier town of New York, pillaged, and massacred the inhabitants, and burned the fort and houses. The second expedition mustered at Three Rivers, and fell on the village called Sementels (or Salmon Falls) in New Hampshire, which it demolished, and in returning fell in with the 3d division, made up in part of Acadian troops, who had mustered at Quebec. Joining forces, they assailed and gained possession of the fortified village of Kaskebé, in Maine, which lay upon the sea. A large convoy was now despatched to Michilimakinac, to strengthen that remote western trading-post, and to conciliate, by presents, the Ottawa and Huron chiefs. The Governor thus secured the fur-trade of a wide region, and restored the influence of the French.

VII.—The New Englanders now resolved on reprisals, and besides sending out a small squadron which took Port Royal and therewith all Acadia, they planned two expeditions against Canada: one by sea from Boston, against Quebec; the other by land from New York, against Montreal. The latter, under General Winthrop, failed through want of necessary stores, conjoined to dissatisfaction among his Indian allies, and fell back without accomplishing anything. The naval force consisted of 32 vessels and nearly 2000 marines, and was led by Sir William Phipps. Several French posts on the coasts of Newfoundland and the lower St. Lawrence were taken with impunity, and the fleet had reached Tadoussac before Frontenac was warned of his danger. He hastened from Montreal, strengthened the defences of Quebec, and refused the Englishman's summons to surrender. Phipps landed about 1500 troops and some field-pieces, but through the activity and

4

courageous zeal of the French he was obliged to desist from his attempts. Considering the enterprise hopeless, he re-embarked the soldiers, leaving his cannon in the hands of the enemy (1690). In Quebec a church was built to commemorate this deliverance, and dedicated to "Notre Dame de la Victoire." Unfortunately it was set on fire by the bursting of a shell, and burned to the ground, during the siege of Quebec by General Wolfe. The French King, on receiving the intelligence of success from the gallant Count, caused a medal to be struck with the words "Francia in novo orbe victrix; Kebeca liberata, A.D., M.D.C.X.C."

In the following year a large body of Iroquois, assisted by the English, advanced along the Richelieu to attack Montreal, but they were repulsed by de Callière. The Governor was now engaged in strengthening the fortifications of Quebec, so as to make it the most formidable stronghold in America. In 1694, the Iroquois were decidedly inclined for peace, and allowed the Governor to re-establish the fort at Cataraqui without hindrance. Still further to impress the Indians, a grand expedition was led forth against some refractory tribes, who, nevertheless, managed to evade the pursuit of the French. The latter, after contenting themselves with burning villages and destroying grain, returned to Montreal.

VIII.—A discussion had now arisen between the Colonial and Home Governments with reference to the advanced trading-posts in the upper parts of Canada. The Court maintained that they were of little use, and were besides a constant cause of war, and proposed that the natives should bring their furs to Montreal, while the attention of the colonists should be entirely devoted to agriculture. But the Governor objected that this step would throw their allies into the hands of the Iroquois, and that all the trade would pass into British channels—while, moreover, a general confederacy of the tribes against France might be reasonably dreaded. His reasons prevailed, and the monopoly of the northern fur-trade, which ensured ample profits, remained with the French. The Colonial war, known as *King William's War*, was now settled by the treaty of peace between England and France, signed at Ryswick in 1697. In the same year, Sieur de Rêvérin formed a company, and established a fishing station at the harbour of Mount Louis, half-way between Quebec and the Gulf.

LOUIS HECTOR DE CALLIÈRE, GOVERNOR, 1699.

IX.—In 1698, the old veteran, Count de Frontenac, died at Quebec, aged 78, and was succeeded by M. de Callière, Commandant of Montreal. In 1701, a temporary pacification and alliance of all the Indian tribes was effected by him. In the same year the War of the Spanish Succession broke out in Europe, in which France and England were engaged on opposite sides, and the latter soon conceived the magnificent design of annexing to herself the whole North American Continent.

PHILIPPE DE RIGAUD, MARQUIS DE VAUDREUIL, GOV., 1703.

In 1703, de Callière died at Quebec, and the colonists petitioned for the appointment of the Marquis de Vaudreuil, which Louis XIV. willingly granted. Soon after his accession to power, a deputation from some of the Iroquois formally acknowledged for the first time the sovereignty of France, and claimed her protection. The number of French now in Canada was over 15,000. It was at this time that the King increased the number of sovereign councillors to twelve. In 1708, a council was held at Montreal to determine on the course to be pursued against the English, who were intriguing with the Indians. The result was that an attack was made by 400 French and Indians on a border fort, named Haverhill, which they carried, and effected a retreat, though not without some loss. In 1709, Col. Vetch laid before Queen Anne a scheme for the conquest of Canada, which was approved of, and a fleet of 20 ships prepared for executing it; but they, being called off to Portugal, never crossed the Atlantic. The English meanwhile had formed a chain of forts from New York to Lakes George and Champlain, on which lakes they then erected forts with a view of covering their descent on Canada. Failing, however, to obtain the co-operation of the Iroquois, who found it most for their interest to remain neutral, they relinquished the design and burned their forts. In 1710 another abortive expedition was undertaken against Canada. A fleet under Sir Hovenden Walker, with seven regiments of Marlborough's troops, was sent from England to co-operate with General Nicholson, who marched, at the head of 4000 militia, from Albany towards the frontier. The fleet, being driven among islands and reefs in the river, was almost entirely destroyed, and Nicholson, hearing of this miscarriage, retraced his steps. The greatest enthusiasm prevailed at Quebec, and on the rumour of another invasion in 1712, the merchants furnished the Governor with 50,000 crowns to strengthen the fortifications of the town. A new enemy now entered the field against the French, in the Outagamis or Foxes, who undertook to destroy the fort at Detroit (a station established in 1701). But the French, assisted by Indian allies, defeated them in a succession of sanguinary engagements, and almost annihilated the tribe. The war, which had been raging continually on the boundaries of the Colonies, and is commonly spoken of as *Queen Anne's war*, was brought to a close, and the alarm of the colonists quieted, in 1713, by the Peace of Utrecht, by which Louis XIV. ceded Acadia, Newfoundland, and Hudson's Bay Territory, together with all claims over the Iroquois, to England. Canada, however, was retained by France.

X.—After the treaty, Canada enjoyed a long period of tranquillity, in which her resources were greatly developed. In 1717 a court of admiralty was established. In 1720 and 1721, Charlevoix, a noted French traveller, visited the colony. Quebec, in the latter year, contained 7000 inhabitants, and Montreal 3000; the population of the entire Colony numbered 25,000, of whom 5000 constituted a provincial militia. The land along the St. Lawrence for some distance below Quebec, was laid out in Seigneuries, and tolerably well cultivated. Above Montreal, which was rapidly rising in importance, there was no extensive settlement, but merely forts at Cataraqui, Niagara, Detroit, and Michilimakinac. In 1722 the Governor, Bishop St. Valier (who succeeded Laval in 1688), and the Intendant Begon divided the country into 82 parishes. About 1717, the Iroquois confederacy was joined by another tribe, the Tuscaroras, from North Carolina, since which time it has consisted of Six Nations, and is so named by English writers. Vaudreuil, after a rule of twenty-two years, died at Quebec, October 10th, 1725.

CHARLES, MARQUIS DE BEAUHARNOIS, GOVERNOR, 1726.

The government was administered by the Baron de Longueuil, a native of Canada, until the appointment of the Marquis de Beauharnois, in 1726, who held office

4*

for twenty years. He diligently promoted the interests of the Colony, and Seigneurial farms were extended along the whole distance from Quebec to Montreal. The Indians generally were now becoming conciliated, both by the suave and obliging manners of the French, and by frequent intermarriage. In 1736, the Colony contained about 40,000 inhabitants.

XI.—The Governor of New York having erected a fort and trading-post at Oswego, with the view of procuring the commerce of the lakes, Beauharnois obtained permission from the Iroquois to construct a French fort at the entrance of the Niagara River, more efficient than the former stockade. The Governor also built a fort on the commanding position of Ticonderoga, and another at Crown Point, on Lake Champlain, which secured the frontier-line. A large annual fair was opened at Montreal, and this place became the centre of the fur-traffic. In 1745, France and England were embroiled in the War of the Austrian Succession, and colonial war followed in consequence. This, however, was confined chiefly to Nova Scotia, and its pernicious effects did not mar the prosperity of Canada. The Marquis de la Jonquière, Admiral of France, was appointed Governor in 1746; but, on the outward voyage, his fleet was intercepted by Admiral Anson and Rear-Admiral Warren. The French were defeated in the engagement which ensued, and the new Governor of Canada was made prisoner. Upon the capture becoming known in France, the Count de la Galissonière was commissioned to fill the vacancy so created.

ROLAND MICHEL BARRIN, COUNT DE LA GALISSONIÈRE, GOVERNOR, 1747.

This nobleman arrived safely in 1747; and although ruling for little more than two years, he thoroughly studied the position of Canada and proposed a measure, on returning to France, which marks his intelligence. He recommended that the frontier, instead of being kept a wilderness, should be peopled by 10,000 peasants fom France, who would thus act as a check upon the invasions of the British. His advice passed unheeded, and the peace of Aix-la-Chapelle in 1748 terminated hostilities for a time. Just before the peace the Governor dispatched M. Céleron de Bienville with 300 men, to define the boundaries of the French Colonial possessions. A line was assumed from Detroit running south-east, to the Ohio, and thence along the Apalachian Mountains; leaden plates, with suitable inscriptions, were buried at intervals to mark out this limit. While La Galissonière was tampering with the Acadians and exciting a revolt against British authority, the Admiral de la Jonquière was released. In 1748 François Bigot was appointed Intendant of all the North American possessions of France.

JACQUES PIERRE DE TAFFANEL, MARQUIS DE LA JONQUIÈRE, GOVERNOR, 1749.

XII.—La Jonquière reached Canada in 1749, whereupon the Count resigned his trust and returned to France. The new Governor took an active share in Nova Scotian affairs, and stopped for a time, by arbitrary seizures, the trading of English merchants on the banks of the Ohio. To neutralize the influence which the English acquired by Fort Oswego, (built in 1722,) he constructed a fort on Lake Ontario, in 1750, called Rouillé (the name of the Minister of Marine) or more frequently Toronto, which occupied the site of the present capital. In the same year Commissioners met at Paris to settle the North American boundaries between England and France, but the French were so exorbitant in their demands that the conference was broken up, without any arrangement being concluded.

In this year the number of colonial inhabitants amounted to 65,000.

A great and growing evil now became manifest in the Canadian Government. The salaries granted to the officials by the Home Government were so scanty that they had every inducement to peculation. Incalculable dishonesty prevailed in the Indian trade, and the finances generally became involved in disorder. The Governor monopolized the sale of brandy to the Indians, and thus realized enormous profits, which gratified his avarice; while the Intendant, Bigot, farmed out trade-licenses, and having, moreover, the distribution of public money for military service, he managed to accumulate during his career fraudulent wealth to the amount of £400,000 sterling. La Jonquière's avarice provoked complaints on the part of the colonists, and fearing an investigation, he demanded his recall. Before a successor could be appointed, the Governor died at Quebec in 1752, and was buried in the Récollet Church, alongside of Frontenac and Vaudreuil, his predecessors. He was replaced temporarily by Charles le Moyne, Baron de Longueuil, (son of him formerly mentioned,) then Governor of Montreal. In this year (1752) two ships laden with wheat were sent to Marseilles, and this was probably the first exportation of Canadian grain.

MARQUIS DUQUESNE DE MENNEVILLE, GOVERNOR, 1752.

XIII.—Before the end of 1752, arrived as Governor General the Marquis Duquesne, who encroached more decidedly than any of his predecessors upon British territory. He first attended to the military resources of the Colony: the Quebec and Montreal militia was organized; companies of artillery were formed; afterwards the militia of the county-parishes was carefully inspected and disciplined. He then equipped detachments, who fortified several posts upon the Ohio and the Alleghanies. The Governor's object was to keep up free communication between Canada and Louisiana, as well as to deprive the English traders, who formed the Ohio Company, of all share in the western fur-trade. The Governor of Virginia thought to check these hostile designs, and sent a body of militia to hold the forks of the Ohio and Monongahela. This company had already commenced the erection of a fort when the French drove them from the position, and completing the fortification, named it Fort Duquesne. Fort Necessity was soon reared in the neighbourhood by Lieutenant-Colonel George Washington, at the head of the Virginia militia. The Iroquois, at this time, equally courted by English and French, endeavoured by every means to remain neutral in the contest. But finding this impossible, they fluctuated from side to side, according to the success of the opposing parties, till finally it became clear to the majority of the warriors, that their interest would be best promoted by adhering unwaveringly to the British flag. In the course of hostilities which ended in 1754, Washington was forced to capitulate to M. de Villiers. Thus began, originating from a question of disputed boundaries, what is commonly called the *French War*, in which England and France subsequently participated by a formal declaration of hostilities in 1756,—a date marking the commencement of the European Seven Years' War.

XIV.—The English Government notified their colonists to unite for common defence, and a Congress was accordingly held at Albany, where a general confederation of the British Colonies was proposed by Benjamin Franklin, but without any practical result. Meanwhile, the Governor of Massachusetts planted forts on the Kennebec river, to secure the north-eastern frontier, and at his solicitations two regiments were ordered from Ireland to unite with the colonists in resisting the encroachments of France. Major-General Braddock, being appointed General of all the British forces in America, arrived in 1755, with strict orders to march upon Fort Duquesne. These he prepared to fulfil in concert with two other expeditions planned by the Council at Albany: the one against Niagara, under Shirley, Governor of Massachusetts; the other under William Johnson against Crown Point. France had now prepared a fleet at Brest under Admiral de la Motte, having on board Baron Dieskau, (who had gained renown under Marshal Saxe,) at the head of six battalions of veteran troops, forming in all 8000 men. Two of these battalions were to be left at Louisburg, the rest were destined for Canada. The Marquis Duquesne, having requested his recall, with a view of reentering the naval service, was succeeded in 1755 by the Marquis de Vaudreuil-Cavagnal, Governor of Louisiana, and the last French Governor of Canada.

PIERRE RIGAUD, MARQUIS DE VAUDREUIL-CAVAGNAL, GOVERNOR, 1755.

This nobleman, son of a former Governor, and born at Quebec in 1698, was appointed in compliance with the wishes of the people, who remembered his father's happy administration of that high office, whereof popular favour had likewise made him the incumbent. De la Motte's fleet reached Quebec with the new Governor in 1755, having lost two of his ships, which were captured off Newfoundland by Admiral Boscawen. The whole Colony was now under arms and agriculture was neglected. Provisions became scarce and prices rose enormously, while the fur-trade was declining. Notwithstanding this, the Intendant, Bigot, and his creatures shipped off wheat to the West Indies, and received large profits. The Governor sanctioned these proceedings and others equally infamous, and soon lost the respect and confidence of the people.

XV.—Meanwhile Braddock's expedition had set forward, but it became entangled in the Alleghany defiles, and was cut to pieces by a Franco-Indian ambuscade, (1755.) The General was mortally wounded, and Washington conducted a masterly retreat. The British frontier was now unprotected, and was ravaged ferociously by the French and their Indian allies. Shirley's expedition against Niagara accomplished nothing beyond strengthening Fort Oswego, and erecting on the opposite side of the river a new fort, named Ontario. Johnson took the field with 6000 militiamen and 800 Iroquois Indians, over which people he exercised almost supreme influence. He erected Fort Edward, near Lake George. The French had entrenched themselves at Ticonderoga, and were reinforced by Dieskau, with some of his regulars, as well as Canadians and Indians. The Baron attacked the British position on Lake George, but was repulsed with heavy loss, and he himself fatally wounded. The French left their General on the field, and sought shelter at Ticonderoga; while Johnson built Fort William Henry on the commanding position he had occupied. The campaign of 1755 had, however, on the whole preponderated in favour of France, and many Indians were on this account forsaking the British, and casting in their lot with the winning party.

XVI.—In 1756, the English Government appointed the Earl of Loudon as Commander-in-chief of its American forces, and the Marquis de Montcalm was nominated to a similar post by Louis XV.; regular troops accompanied each General to the scene of action. In August, Montcalm gained possession of Fort Ontario and Fort Oswego, and caused both to be demolished. This brilliant success was stained by the barbarous murder of many English prisoners by Montcalm's Indians. On the western frontier, innumerable murders and massacres of English colonists were being continually perpetrated by the savages, aided by scarcely less savage Canadians. In the whole campaign success remained on the side of the French; by destroying Oswego, they gained the unhindered control of Lakes Ontario and Erie, and the English forfeited the Indian trade and commerce of the western lakes. After an ineffectual attempt by a brother of the Governor Vaudreuil upon Fort William Henry, it was obliged to capitulate to the victorious Montcalm. Again, in spite of the General's efforts, the blood-thirsty Indians fell upon the English garrison and slaughtered over 1000 men (1757). This important fort was dismantled, and all the English vessels were destroyed on Lake George, the command of which passed into the hands of the French. Even Johnson's entreaties could hardly restrain the whole Iroquois Nation, at this juncture, from going over to the side of the victors.

XVII.—A change of ministry occurred at this time in England, and the great Commoner, William Pitt, was placed at the helm of Government. In 1758 the first operations were directed against Nova Scotia and Cape Breton, which obtained signal success in the capture of Louisburg (the key of the St. Lawrence) by the exertions of Admiral Boscawen, General Amherst, and Brigadier-General *Wolfe*. A squadron was then sent round to break up the French settlements on the Gulf and River St. Lawrence. Many fishing-stations were destroyed, and among the rest that at Mount Louis. The current of war, with one exception, now set in favour of England until the close of the contest—an auspicious change for which gratitude is due to the energy of the great war-minister, Pitt. The inefficient and vacillating General Loudon was recalled, and the chief command fell to Abercromby; the British cabinet pledged itself to repair at any cost the losses of the colonists, and called upon them to come forward in the common cause —a summons which was willingly obeyed by all. The second expedition was planned against Ticonderoga and Crown Point.

The largest army seen in America, consisting of 6350 regulars and 9000 militia, assembled at Albany, and advanced towards these strong positions, which commanded the chain of waters leading to the St. Lawrence and into the very heart of Canada. Montcalm, therefore, resolved to defend these "Gates of Canada" with all his resources. Abercromby, after Lord Howe had been killed in a skirmish, drew his army aside with some pusillanimity, and attacked the French encampment at Carillon, close by Ticonderoga. Here he was terribly defeated and 2000 of his men slain. This great misfortune was in some measure repaired by the adventurous Bradstreet, who captured Fort Frontenac, containing immense stores of provisions and ammunition for the supply of Fort Duquesne and the western forts. This post was laid in ruins, and then abandoned by the British. The third and last great expedition against Fort Duquesne was led by General Forbes, in November. This stronghold was not in a position to resist; the French Commander therefore abandoned it, and floated down the Ohio to a friendly settlement. The British thereupon took possession, repaired the fort, and substituted for its former name that of Pittsburg, in honour of the celebrated minister. This conquest was of great advantage in protecting the western frontier, and in reviving respect among the Indians, who began to proffer help in some cases, and in others, neutrality, to the British. In fact the reduction of the two forts Frontenac and Duquesne, insured to England the whole territory from the Canadian lakes to the Gulf of Mexico, for the possession of which this war had arisen. On the news of this campaign reaching England, Abercromby was superseded by Amherst the conqueror of Louisburg, as Generalissimo of the Anglo-American troops.

XVIII.—In 1759, Pitt's scheme of uniting the French territories in America with those of England, thus creating one vast range of dominion, was drawing nigh its realization. A comprehensive plan, similar in its general features to that of the previous year's campaign, was arranged, whereby Canada was to be attacked simultaneously at three different points—Niagara, Montreal, and Quebec—by military and naval operations combined. But this plan was subsequently modified, inasmuch as its execution was found to be impracticable. The Marquis de Vaudreuil perceived that the object of England was the annihilation of French power in America, and issued a proclamation to quicken the zeal of the Canadian militia. He directed that all males, from sixteen to sixty, should be enrolled as soldiers, and ready to march at the shortest notice. The result of a census showed 15,229 as the number of those capable of bearing arms, but a large proportion were neither serviceable nor trustworthy. The rapacity of the government in seizing the colonists' grain, to profit by the sale of it, had brought on the greatest distress, and indeed absolute famine, so that horses were used for food in Quebec and Montreal. M. de Bougainville was dispatched to France to crave succour and reinforcements, but returned without success. Montcalm strengthened, as far as possible, the various outposts and outlying settlements, and appointed his officers to their several commands.

XIX.—In July 1759, General Amherst moved against Ticonderoga first, and then Crown Point, both which after sharp fighting were evacuated by the French, who retired to Isle aux Noix, which commanded the Richelieu. Amherst occupied the forts, and was here delayed until winter stopped all proceedings without being able to attack the enemy, for want of transports. In the same month, Brigadier Prideaux and Sir William Johnson (knighted for the victory over Baron Dieskau, 1755) with his Indians, marched against Fort Niagara. Prideaux was killed by the bursting of a mortar, but the investment was carried on skilfully by Johnson. He defeated the army of relief under d'Aubry, and this last chance of succour having vanished, the garrison capitulated on honourable terms (July 25). In February, a fleet under Admiral Saunders sailed from England for Quebec, and to Wolfe, now raised to the rank of Major-General, was assigned the chief command. They touched at Nova Scotia for reinforcements, so that finally the number of land forces on board was about 8000. On June 27th the troops were landed on the island of Orleans. Within Quebec was the valiant Montcalm at the head of 12,000 French and Canadian troops. A British brigade under Monckton was now shipped across the arm of the river, and drove the Canadians from Point Levi, opposite Quebec, whence heavy ordnance could be played upon the besieged city. Strong intrenchments were thrown up on the western extremity of Orleans. The British fleet then opened their guns upon the enemy's lines between Quebec and the Falls of Montmorency, and under the cover of the fire Wolfe landed on the north shore below the Falls, and intrenched his position.

But there was no ford across the river, and an error had been committed by Wolfe in dividing his small army. While Saunders occupied his original position off Orleans, a squadron under Holmes had been sent up the river to harass the French above Quebec and to reconnoitre. Wolfe had now been five weeks before Quebec, and as yet no important result had been gained. He then attempted the desperate measure of forcing the French intrenchments above the Montmorency at Beauport, but he was beaten back with a loss of 450 men.

XX.—While Wolfe lay on a sick bed, a council of war was called, and Colonel Townshend proposed the skilfully-audacious plan which was adopted by all. Above Quebec, a narrow path had been discovered winding up the precipitous cliff, 300 feet high; this was to be secretly ascended, and the Heights of Abraham gained, which overlook the city. Part of the British fleet, containing that portion of the army which had occupied the northern shore, sailed past Quebec to Cap-Rouge (Sept. 12), and there joined Holmes. The rest of the troops marched up the south shore till they arrived opposite the men-of-war. Here embarking in flat-bottomed boats, they dropped down the river the same night to Wolfe's cove, and almost unopposed, division after division scaled the heights. When morning dawned, Wolfe's whole disposable force, in number 4828, with one small gun, was ranged in battle-array upon the Plains of Abraham.

Meanwhile, Montcalm had been completely deceived by the tactics of the British General. He had dispatched M. de Bougainville with nearly 2000 men to oppose the British at Cap-Rouge, where he thought they intended to land; while he himself watched the movements of Saunders, who made a feint of landing at

Beauport. Moreover, in the French camp, there was a want of unanimity: half-famished Canadians were deserting every day, and mutual distrust had arisen between Montcalm and the Governor. On seeing the true state of affairs, the French General crossed the St. Charles, and seized by some incomprehensible impulse, determined to meet Wolfe in the open field. He accordingly attacked the British force (Sept. 13) with *1759* 7520 men, besides Indians, and two pieces of artillery. In the desperate struggle which followed, both Wolfe and Montcalm were mortally wounded; but complete victory at last remained in the hands of the British. The loss on the side of the conquerors amounted to 55 killed and 607 wounded; that of the French is uncertain, but was probably about 1500 in killed wounded and prisoners. Scarcely was the battle of the Plains of Abraham over, when Bougainville appeared with his forces,—but only to retreat with great precipitation. Four days afterwards, a flag of truce came from the city, and the day following, (Sept 18, 1759,) *Quebec capitulated.* Before night, floated from the walls of this American Gibraltar the broad banner of England, where it has ever since remained untouched by an enemy's hand. The garrison was allowed to march out with the honours of war, and was then to be embarked and sent to the nearest port in France. Wolfe died on the field of battle; his remains were conveyed to England and interred in Greenwich. Montcalm died on the 14th, and was buried within the precincts of the Ursuline Convent at Quebec.

XXI.—The remains of the French forces, with the Governor, had meanwhile assembled at Montreal, and Chevalier de Levi assumed the command. In the spring they moved down to attack Quebec, upwards of 10,000 strong. General Murray, who commanded at Quebec,

5*

unwarned by Montcalm's fate, met this force on the Heights of St. Foy with scarcely 3000 men. He was defeated with great loss, and retired within the walls. Levi prepared to besiege the city; but on the approach of the British fleet, he withdrew. Lake Ontario was now cleared of French cruisers; and the combined British army, nearly 10,000 strong, under Amherst and Johnson, moved down upon Montreal, where the strength of the French was centred. Murray, with 2500 men, sailed from Quebec to co-operate with Amherst. Colonel Haviland, also, with over 2000 troops, who had driven the French from Isle aux Noix, now bore down upon the same fated town—so that 16,000 British were before Montreal. On the 8th September, 1760, the Marquis de Vaudreuil, on terms similar to those granted at Quebec, signed the capitulation which transferred Canada, from the Gulf of St. Lawrence to the unknown western wilds, into the hands of England. Canada was formally ceded to the British crown by the Treaty of Paris, Feb. 10th, 1763.

QUESTIONS TO CHAPTER IV.

I. Who was the first Governor under the new régime, and when appointed? What procured his recall? Where did he die? Who succeeded him, and with what titles? What other officials accompanied the Marquis de Tracy? What regiment now came? In what year were sheep and horses introduced? What measures were taken against the Iroquois, and with what effect? Describe the French expedition against the Indians. What became of the officers of the regiment? What did the viceroy do before returning? Who was the next Governor, and in what year? What was the population in this year? What peace was concluded, and how long did it last?

II. What travels were now undertaken, and by whom? With what result? Where was a site for a fort fixed upon? Why did the Governor resign? What disease broke out among the Indians, and with what result?

III. Who followed M. de Courcelles? What fort was built, and how named? What scheme of exploration planned, and by whom? Who discovered the Mississippi? What induced La Salle to go to France? What did he effect in that country? What did he do on arriving in Canada? Who joined his expedition, and in what capacity? Describe the first vessel built in Canada. Where did La Salle establish trading-posts? What became of the Griffon?

QUESTIONS TO CHAPTER IV.

How far did La Salle journey? What country did he take possession of, and in whose name?

IV. What was Frontenac's character? Why was he recalled? By whom succeeded, and in what year? What was the population now? What circumstances gave rise to hostilities between the French and Iroquois? Why did the Iroquois disregard the complaints of the French? What policy did this people endeavour to pursue? What reinforcement did the Governor now receive? What did he determine upon? Describe his expedition against the Indians. What mortified him on reaching Quebec?

V. By whom, and why, was La Barre replaced? How did Denonville act? What letter did he receive in 1686? What dishonourable action did he commit? Where was a fort erected, and what became of it? What attacks did the Iroquois make? What interrupted the peace? What resulted? What were the virtual limits of French Canada at this time?

VI. Who was made Governor in 1689? How were the Indians pacified? Why did Frontenac make an attack upon the English? What war was now going on between France and England? Mention Frontenac's expeditions. Describe their results. Where was a convoy sent, and for what purpose?

VII. What expeditions were undertaken by the New Englanders? Give an account of them. What commemorated the deliverance of Quebec? How did the French King act on receiving news of the victory? What action occurred on the part of the Iroquois? Describe the French expedition against the Indians.

VIII. What discussion had arisen between the Colonial and Home Governments? State the arguments which prevailed. By what name was this war commonly spoken of, and how was it ended? Where was a fishing-station established, and by whom?

IX. Where and when did Frontenac die? By whom succeeded? What war now broke out in Europe, and in what year? What occasioned the Marquis de Vaudreuil's appointment? What remarkable Iroquois deputation came to him? Give the number of French in Canada. Why was a council held at Montreal? What was the result of its deliberations? What plan was laid before Anne in 1709, and by whom? What was the effect? Where had the English formed posts? How did their design result? Describe the English expedition of 1710. How did the merchants show their enthusiasm at Quebec? What new enemy had the French? What success had they? What was this colonial war commonly called, and how was it ended? What did Louis XIV. cede at peace of Utrecht?

X. What was the condition of Canada after the treaty? What traveller visited the country, and in what years? What was the population of Quebec, and of the whole colony? How many militiamen? What settlements above Montreal? How long did Vaudreuil govern? When and where did he die? What change took place in the Iroquois confederacy? Who was the next Governor, and who administered till he arrived? Where were farms extended? How were the Indians becoming conciliated? What was the population in 1736?

XI. Why was a fort constructed at Niagara? At what other points were forts built? How was the fur-trade promoted? What war broke out in 1745? In what place was the colonial war confined? What prevented La Jonquière from fulfilling his appointment in 1746? On his capture, who was appointed? What measure marks La Galissoniere's intelligence? By what peace and in what year was the war ended? What did the Governor do just before the peace? Give the boundary assumed by France. With what people did the Governor tamper? Who was now appointed Intendant?

XII. Who was the next Governor? What were his acts on arriving? What fort did he construct, and for what reason? Describe the events at Paris. What was the population now? State the great evil in the Canadian Government. Exemplify it. Why did the Governor ask for his recall? When did he die? What Governors were buried in the Récollet church? Who governed temporarily? Mention the first exportation of Canadian grain.

XIII. Who encroached on the British territory? To what did he first give attention? Mention circumstances. Where did he fortify posts, and with what objects? Who opposed him, and in what way? Describe the erection of Fort Duquesne. What fort was built in the neighbourhood, and by whom? State the policy of the Iroquois. To whom did Washington capitulate? From what did the French war originate? What European war began in 1756?

XIV. For what purpose was the Albany congress held? What scheme was proposed, and by whom? What did the Governor of Massachusetts effect? Who was appointed British General, and when did he arrive? What were his orders? What other expeditions were formed? What help came from France? Who was the last French Governor of Canada? Why was he appointed? When and how did he arrive? Exemplify his bad government.

XV. Give the results of Braddock's expedition. What did Shirley effect? Describe Johnson's campaign. What was the position of affairs in 1755?

XVI. Who were the colonial commanders in 1756? What was Montcalm's first success? What were the results of this campaign? What fort was next taken? What followed? Give the general results.

XVII. What change took place in England? Where were the operations begun? With what success? How was the Mount Louis fishing-station destroyed? What changes did Pitt produce in American affairs? Sketch the second expedition. How was Abercromby's defeat in some measure repaired? Against what place was the third expedition directed? How did this fort get the name by which it is now known? What was gained by reducing Frontenac and Duquesne? Who replaced Abercromby, and in what capacity?

XVIII. What was Pitt's scheme? What was the proposed plan of operations? What were the measures of the French Governor? What was the number of Canadian militia? To what state was the colony reduced? How was Montcalm employed?

XIX. State General Amherst's movements. Who led the expedition against Niagara? With what success? When did the English fleet sail, and under what commanders? What was the number of English troops? Of French troops in Quebec? What places were occupied by the English? Where did Wolfe land? What was his error? What desperate measure was attempted? With what result?

XX. Who proposed the plan finally adopted? State this plan. How was it accomplished? What was the number of Wolfe's men? How had Montcalm been deceived? What want of unanimity was then in Quebec? When did Montcalm attack, and with what force? Who gained the victory? What loss on both sides? What was the battle called? Who appeared after it was over? When did Quebec capitulate? What conditions were granted to the garrison? Where were Wolfe and Montcalm buried?

XXI. Where did the French assemble? Who took the command? What were their movements in the spring? Where was Murray defeated? Why did Levi withdraw? What forces now bore down on Montreal? When was the capitulation of Canada signed? When was Canada formally ceded to England?

PART II.—~~CANADA~~ ~~UNDER~~ ~~THE~~ ~~BRITISH.~~

CHAPTER I.

FROM THE OVERTHROW OF FRENCH DOMINION IN CANADA TO THE DIVISION OF THE PROVINCE INTO UPPER AND LOWER CANADA.

I.—On the capitulation of Canada in 1760, the French population was estimated at 69,275 (excluding over 3000 soldiers and others who had gone back to France) and the converted Indians at 7400. The British guaranteed to the colony the free exercise of the Roman Catholic religion, and the preservation of property and privileges belonging to the religious communities; but this was refused to the Jesuits, the Franciscans and the Sulpicians. Immunity was to be granted to the colonists for their share in the war, and they were to have accorded to them the same civil and commercial privileges as British subjects. The Indians friendly to France were also to remain unmolested in the possession of their lands.

At this time were disclosed the enormous frauds and embezzlements of the French officials during the late war and previous thereunto. Many of the inhabitants were ruined by the refusal of the French government at home to honour the bills drawn and the paper-currency issued by the late Intendant, Bigot, to the extent, it is said, of over £3,000,000 sterling. Bigot, on his return to France, was thrown into the Bastille, and was afterwards condemned to perpetual banishment.

II.—A short time after the conquest and under

Murray's administration, there was a comprehensive scheme formed by an Indian chief named Pontiac, belonging to the Ottawa tribe, for the overthrow of the British, and their total expulsion from the country. No plan ever framed by the Indians can rival this in the breadth of its conception or in the vigour and systematic perseverance of its prosecution. Pontiac was born about 1714, and early allied himself with the French, to whom he constantly adhered afterwards. He was present in nearly all the important actions between the French and the English colonists in their struggle for supremacy. On the ultimate triumph of the latter, he contemplated a simultaneous attack upon all their frontier posts from the Niagara to Lake Michigan. These military stations were ten in number; at Niagara, at Presqu' Isle, at La Bœuf, at Pittsburg, at Sandusky, at the Miamis, at Detroit, at Michilimackinac, at Green Bay, and at St. Joseph. He succeeded in capturing seven of these; but Niagara, Detroit, and Pittsburg were impregnable to his assaults. The siege of Pittsburg is the most extraordinary passage in the annals of Indian campaigning. A British armed vessel was taken by a fleet of canoes, while the siege commenced in May 1763, was carried on till the place was relieved by General Bradstreet in 1764. Pontiac's efforts, therefore, to dispossess the British, were futile, and he at last fled the country, and took refuge among the Indians on the Illinois, where he was subsequently assassinated in a petty quarrel.

III.—General Amherst, before departing to New York, regulated the government of the country, and as Governor General left instructions to his lieutenants. Canada was divided into three districts and placed under military courts. General Murray governed at Quebec; General Gage at Montreal, and Colonel Burton at Three Rivers. At the capital the most important civil and criminal affairs were decided by the commandant, assisted by a military council composed of about seven officers, which sat twice a week. General Gage was rather more liberal, and allowed the people in certain cases to settle their own disputes with right of appeal to the military ruler of the district. He afterwards erected five courts of justice, where officers of the French Canadian militia decided on the causes of their compatriots. The government at Three Rivers was nearly as arbitrary as that of Quebec. The Canadians regarded this military régime as a violation of the terms of capitulation which insured to them the rights of British subjects; but they were pacified by the assurance that, on the conclusion of peace between the European powers, a regular civil government would be established. For over three years after the conquest martial law was predominant. In October, 1763, George III., by royal proclamation, virtually abolished the French laws and substituted those of England, and it was announced that representative assemblies should be convoked only when circumstances permitted. In November of the same year, Murray was named Governor General, as successor to Lord Amherst, who returned to Europe. The Governor called together a new council, which was invested, in common with himself, with executive, legislative, and judiciary powers. The right to impose taxes alone was withheld. The council consisted of the two Lieutenant-Governors at Montreal and Three Rivers, the Chief Justice, the Inspector General, and eight of the most noted inhabitants. Only one French Canadian found place in this council; an invidious distinction which, being persevered in, gave rise to many subsequent troubles. The Court of King's Bench and that of Common Pleas were now established, the judges of which were nominated by a majority of the council. In April, 1766, the Governor and a special council established in Quebec a system of equity jurisdiction, which was, in fact, the introduction of the Court of Chancery into Canada. In 1764, the Governor was appointed vice-Admiral in the province of Quebec, and the territories thereon depending; a title which his successors yet retain.

IV.—In 1763 a printing-press was brought from Philadelphia by a Mr. Brown, and the first newspaper in Canada, named the "Quebec Gazette," appeared on June 21st, 1764, being partly in French and partly in English. This journal is yet in existence as a tri-weekly English paper. The first Montreal paper, also called "The Gazette," and printed in French, followed the former, in 1778. In 1765, a great fire broke out in Montreal, which consumed one hundred and eight houses; and three years after another occurred which burned ninety houses to the ground. All official appointments were now conferred upon British-born subjects and Protestants, selected from the officers of the army and the traders, who at that time represented in great part this class of the population. These officials too frequently showed undue contempt and superciliousness to the *new subjects*, (as the Canadians were called,) and especially to the colonial noblesse. Discontent and disorder were thus produced among the old inhabitants, and we find the annals of Canada to contain at that time little else than a series of petty contests between the old French colonists and the new settlers of British origin. Governor Murray, be it said to his honour, uniformly supported the cause of the French Canadians, and rescued them from many indignities. Even now, however, the decisive change of Canada under French and British rule became marked:

under the former the country had been a military and trading colony, and in time of war the various posts were transformed into a chain of barracks; under the latter, the agricultural element predominated, and as an evidence of this it may be noted that in 1771, 471,000 bushels of wheat were exported, chiefly from the Sorel district.

A representative assembly was allowed to convene once or twice on petition from the people, but only as a mere matter of form. In one of these assemblies Murray allowed Roman Catholics to sit, whereupon arose loud accusation from the British population, which reached the ears of the home government. Murray went to England to defend himself, which he did effectually, but although acquitted of all blame he did not return to Canada. In 1766, Brigadier-General Sir Guy Carleton was appointed Governor, and the severity of colonial rule was somewhat relaxed. Reports were now made under the direction of the home government respecting the administration of justice and the state of Canadian affairs generally. In 1770 these reports were transmitted to England, whither Carleton also repaired to state his views, leaving Cramahé, the President of the Council, at the head of the Government. The English ministry considered the documents, and Thurlow (Attorney General) and Wedderburne (Solicitor General) recommended the plan which was adopted and introduced into Canada in 1774.

V.—In this year a new order of things was instituted by the British government, with the twofold object of tranquillizing the French in view of the apprehended contest with the Thirteen States, and of encouraging British immigration. An act was passed, called "the Quebec Act," which enlarged the boundaries of the province, by including within it all lands in the back

6

settlements, not otherwise possessed by virtue of a previous grant or charter. By the provisions of this bill, all controversies relating to property and civil rights arising among the new subjects, or between them and the British colonists, were to be settled by the old French laws, as in force at the conquest, including herein the custom of Paris and the edicts of the Kings of France and of the colonial Intendants. Judges were to be selected from colonists conversant with those laws, and it was directed that the French language should be used in the courts of justice. In all criminal cases, however, the criminal law of England (and trial by jury) was to be in force. Moreover a council was to be appointed by the Crown, of not more than twenty-three nor less than seventeen members, which was to assist the Governor in framing ordinances for the good government of the Province of Quebec. Legislative powers, subject to the approval of the Crown, were entrusted to the Governor and Council in all matters except in such as related to provincial taxation, and these remained in the power of the home government. An equality of civil rights, also, was granted to both Protestants and Roman Catholics, by that oath being dispensed with which had hitherto precluded the latter from holding office.

Another less important measure was passed in the British House at the same time, providing a revenue for the Colonial Government, by imposing duties on spirits and molasses; this, however, was found to be inadequate, and the deficit was supplied from the imperial treasury.

VI.—These constitutional changes had the effect of quieting Canadian disturbances, and of rendering the inhabitants well satisfied under the established state of affairs, so that they made no response to the inflammatory calls from the Thirteen English Colonies to the south. On September 5, 1774, the first American Congress met at Philadelphia to memorialize the British Government, and amongst many other addresses, one was directed to the people of Canada, inviting their co-operation. The proposal was fruitless; and in September, 1775, the American insurgents determined upon a double invasion of Canada, by way of Lake Champlain and the Kennebec River. Two or three thousand men were assembled on Lake Champlain, under the command of General Montgomery, (once serving under Wolfe,) who proceeded to besiege Forts Chambly and St. John's, which he took after a lengthened resistance, and made prisoners of the garrison. Ethan Allen, an officer commanding under Montgomery, with a detachment, made an attempt to surprise Montreal, but he was met by a small British force, who defeated his troops, and he himself being captured, was sent to England in irons. Meanwhile, Colonel Benedict Arnold setting out from Maine with over 1000 men, ascended the Kennebec, and after many perils and distresses, (so that even dogs were devoured for food by his men,) reached Point Levi, opposite Quebec, on 9th November. His passage over the river being delayed through want of canoes, and owing also to Colonel Maclean's promptitude of movement, Arnold failed in surprising the city. Thereafter, he marched up the north shore of the river, and fixed his station at Pointe aux Trembles. Governor Carleton, who could only muster a small force of French militia in addition to his 800 British troops, was now at Montreal; but, on hearing of Arnold's movements, he resolved to repair to the defence of his capital. This he accomplished under cover of night, and Montgomery immediately occupied Montreal, (November 19.) The American general soon proceeded thence down the river, and having effected a junction with Arnold, the united army under Montgomery's chief command marched against Quebec, now to be assaulted for the fifth time.

VII.—The Governor had under arms no more than 1800 men, made up of 70 regulars, 230 of Fraser's Highland settlers, and the remainder militiamen and mariners. The summons to surrender was, however, rejected, and Montgomery laid siege to the stronghold during the month of December, but without any success. A night-attack was at length determined upon, and orders were issued to prepare for storming the city, before dawn on the last day of the year, (1775.) Two divisions being made of the besieging army, they were led on during a heavy fall of snow—the one headed by Arnold, the other by Montgomery. The attack was made upon opposite sides of Quebec, but the British were prepared. Montgomery's men were mowed down by a tremendous fire of grape-shot, and he himself was killed; while Arnold's division, after gaining some slight success, was attacked in the rear by a detachment from the city, and 426 men were compelled to surrender. Arnold having received a severe wound, had already quitted the field. The Americans had about 100 men killed and wounded; the British less than twenty. Arnold was now appointed to the chief command in Canada, by order of Congress, and the blockade (at the distance of three miles from the walls) was nominally continued during the winter.

In April 1776, Arnold retired in disgust to Montreal, after being superseded by General Wooster, who, arriving with reinforcements, made some further fruitless attempts upon the city. Early in May three ships hove in sight, precursors of a larger fleet from England, with troops and supplies, on which the enemy raised the siege and hastily retreated. They were pursued by the newly-arrived British under General Burgoyne, who captured one division of the Americans at the Cedars, while another was defeated at Three Rivers, and the rest driven in confusion beyond Lake Champlain. The province was finally evacuated on June 18th, and with the exception of a contemplated expedition under La Fayette, no farther attempt was conceived against Canada. Burgoyne afterwards took Ticonderoga from the Americans, but having encountered General Gates near Saratoga, he met with a severe reverse, and was obliged to capitulate with nearly 6000 troops in October, 1777. In 1778 Carleton departed for England, and was replaced by General Haldimand as Lieutenant-Governor.

VIII.—The peace of Versailles (January 20, 1783), whereby the Independence of the Thirteen United States was recognized, brought to a close this long war between Britain and her colonies. By this treaty the boundaries of Canada were curtailed, so that Quebec and Montreal were within a few leagues of the frontiers; Lake Champlain and the mountains adjoining, as well as Detroit, passed away from the hands of the British. During the progress of the Revolution the population of Canada had received considerable additions from a minority in the States who remained loyal to England. Many thousands of these sought refuge in this country, and under the name of the United Empire Loyalists were commended to the special favour of the provincial government. They received liberal grants of land in Upper Canada, together with farming implements, materials for building, and subsistence for two years, as well as the promise of two hundred acres of free land to be given to each of their children on attaining majority.

At the close of the struggle the province received another accession of inhabitants in the families of many discharged soldiers, who settled in the neighbourhood of Prescott, around the Bay of Quinté, and along the shore of Lake Ontario. Grants were made to these veterans in the following proportions: 5000 acres to field officers; 3000 to captains; 2000 to subalterns; and 200 to privates. This arrangement was subsequently modified, so that the most extensive grant did not exceed 1200 acres. The number of inhabitants in Canada in 1783 was about 125,000, whereof 10,000 or 12,000 loyal refugees had settled in Canada West or Upper Canada, thus laying the foundation of its future prosperity. In 1784, Lieut-Gov. Haldimand established the Iroquois on the banks of the Grand River, between Lakes Erie and Ontario, and also upon the Thames. The last public act of this Governor was to confirm an order of the legislative council whereby the law of Habeas Corpus was introduced, after which he transferred the reins of power to Henry Hamilton, a member of the council (1785.) Hamilton gave place next year to Colonel Hope, Commander-in-chief, who was shortly after (in Oct. 1786) superseded by General Carleton, now raised to the peerage under the name of Lord Dorchester.

In 1787 Canada was visited by a scion of royalty, in the Duke of Clarence, then in command of the 84 gunship *Pegasus*. He afterwards ascended the English throne as William IV. In 1788 Lord Dorchester divided Western Canada into four districts, which he named Lunenburg, Mecklenburg, Nassau, and Hesse. The order of the Jesuits had been abolished in 1762, and in 1788 all their goods were declared to be held subject to the order of the King.

IX.—In a few years the dissimilarity of British and French habits, customs, and notions of government began to be felt. However loyal each party might be to the existing government, yet this alliance was found to be uncongenial. The two distinct codes of legal procedure also contributed to the alienation of each body of colonists from the other. And by recent acts, moreover, the different tenure of land above and below Montreal suggested the propriety of political separation: to the West the land was held in free and common soccage; to the East the feudal tenure prevailed. These things induced William Pitt, son of the Earl of Chatham, to consider the advisability of a division of the province and the grant of a constitution to each community. Meanwhile the country was steadily advancing in prosperity, but yet desires were often strongly expressed, and petitions presented by the British colonists for a representative government. Accordingly, Pitt's scheme, somewhat modified by a suggestion of Fox, and after some opposition both in the English Parliament and from Canadian merchants, passed into law a few years after, and is now spoken of as "The Constitutional Act of 1791." All the other British colonies have had their constitutions granted to them by royal charter; Canada alone by act of Parliament.

X.—By this the Province of Quebec was divided into Upper and Lower Canada, by means of a line running from a point on Lake St. Francis, along the west boundary of the Seigneuries of New Longueuil and Vaudreuil to Point Fortune on the Ottawa, and thence up the river to Lake Temiscaming. It was provided that a Legislative Council and Assembly should be established in each province. The Council was to be composed of life-members chosen by the King (Pitt had proposed a hereditary noblesse): in Upper Canada to consist of not less than seven, in Lower Canada of not less than fifteen gentlemen. Each province was to be divided into electoral districts, which were to return representatives to the Legislative Assemblies;—the limits of the districts and the number of members returned to be defined by the Governor-General. In Upper Canada the members of the Assembly were not to be less than sixteen; in Lower Canada not <u>less than fifty</u>. All laws required to be sanctioned by the two Houses of Assembly and the Governor, before coming into force. There was also for each an Executive Council, consisting of the Governor, and a Cabinet of eleven nominated by the King.

QUESTIONS TO CHAPTER I.

I. What was the population of Canada at the time of its capitulation? How many returned to France? State the nature of the terms granted by the British. What was now disclosed? How were many people ruined? What was Bigot's fate?

II. Who formed a comprehensive scheme? With what design? When was Pontiac born, and to what side did he adhere? State the circumstances of his plan. What military stations did he attack, and with what success? Where was the most remarkable Indian siege carried on? Give some incidents connected with it. At what time did the siege begin, and how was it ended? What was Pontiac's fate?

III. Who was the first English Governor-General of Canada? How did he divide the country? How was it ruled at first, and by whom? State how affairs were managed at Quebec. At Montreal. At Three Rivers. How was this régime regarded by the Canadians? How were they quieted? How long did martial law prevail? What proclamation did George III. make? Who succeeded Amherst, and when? How was the government now conducted? Who composed the Council? What invidious distinction was made? What courts were erected, and how were the judges appointed? What system was established in 1766? What new title did the Governor receive?

IV. When and where did the first Canadian newspaper appear? When was the first Montreal paper published? Mention the great fires at Montreal. To whom were official appointments exclusively given? What was the result? What were the French Canadians now called? How may the history of this time be summed up? How did Murray act? What change distinguishes French from British rule in Canada? How much wheat was exported in 1771? What occasioned Murray to go to England? Who succeeded him, and when? What action did the home-government take? When and why did Carleton go to England? Who recommended a judicious plan? When was it introduced into Canada?

V. Why was a new order of things introduced? What act was now passed? How was Canada enlarged? Define the changes introduced in the legal code. What body was appointed to assist the Governor? What powers were granted to the Governor and Council, and what withheld? What was done respecting religious disqualifications? What was the other measure now passed?

VI. What was the effect of these changes? When did the first American Congress meet? What was its action? When and by what ways did the Americans determine to invade Canada? Who besieged forts Chambly and St. John's, and with what result? Who attempted to surprise Montreal, and with what success? Sketch the movements of Arnold's expedition. Where was Carleton, and what was his action? When and by whom was Montreal occupied? By whom was Quebec now assaulted? How many times previously had it been besieged?

VII. What was the Governor's force? How long did Montgomery besiege? When was a night-attack made? Describe the success of it. What was the loss on both sides? Who succeeded to the command? In what manner was the blockade continued? When did Arnold retire, and on what account? What caused the siege to be ultimately raised? What became of the American army? When was the province evacuated? Who afterwards contemplated a Canadian expedition? What was Burgoyne's fate? What change occurred in the government at this time?

VIII. How and when was this war closed? State how the Canadian boundaries were curtailed. How had the Canadian population been increased during the progress of the revolution? By what name were these refugees known? In what manner were they favoured by the Provincial Government? Who came into Canada at the close of the contest? Where did these soldiers settle? In what proportion were grants of land made to them? How was this arrangement afterwards modified? What was the population of Canada in 1788? What was the number settled in Upper Canada? Where were the Iroquois established, and by whom? What was Haldimand's last act? Name his successor. State the next changes in the government. Who visited Canada in 1787? What division of western Canada was made, and by whom, in 1788? What is said of the Jesuits?

IX. What became felt in a few years? What contributed to the alienation? What suggested political separation? How was the land held to the east and west of Montreal? Who first considered this question, and with what design? What did the British colonists desire? What name is now given to Pitt's scheme? What opposition did it meet with? What distinguishes these constitutions from those granted to other British colonies?

X. How was the Province divided? What was to be established in each Province? Of whom was the Council to be composed? What was Pitt's suggestion? How many members for each Province? How was each Province to be divided? What was the Governor-General to define? How many members for Upper Canada? How many for Lower Canada? After whose sanction did laws come into force? Of whom was the Executive composed?

CHAPTER II.

FROM THE DIVISION OF THE PROVINCE INTO UPPER AND LOWER CANADA TO THE RE-UNION UNDER ONE GOVERNMENT.

I.—CANADA now found herself in possession of the fourth form of government within the short space of thirty-two years. From 1760 to 1763 she was ruled by martial law; from 1763 to 1774 a tyrannical military government prevailed; from 1774 to 1791 a civil government of the most despotic cast was established; and in 1792 a new constitution was introduced, establishing freedom of election and responsibility to the people, which affords a favourable contrast to the illiberal and arbitrary systems that preceded it, wherein the people had not been, in reality, admitted to the slightest share of political privilege. At the time of the separation of the Province east and west of the Ottawa, into French and British divisions, the population of Lower Canada was over 130,000; that of Upper Canada less than 50,000. In August 1791, Prince Edward, father of her present Majesty, arrived at Quebec in command of the Royal Fusiliers, whence he departed in November 1793.

On December 17, 1792, the first Parliament of Lower Canada, consisting of the Legislative Assembly with fifty members, and the Legislative Council with fifteen, was convened at Quebec by Lieutenant-Governor Colonel Clarke, in the absence of Lord Dorchester. On the same day Lieutenant-Governor General Simcoe opened the first Upper Canadian Parliament, consisting of the Legislative Assembly with sixteen, and the Legislative Council with seven members, at Newark, (now Niagara.) By an act of this latter Parliament, Dorchester's names of the four Upper Canadian districts were changed into Eastern, Midland, Home, and Western. There was also an act passed for the building of a gaol and court-house in each of the said districts. The English civil and criminal law and trial by jury were introduced by provincial statute during the session of this Parliament in 1792.

UPPER CANADA, FROM 1792 TO 1812.

II.—Simcoe gave to the River Thames this name, and selected on it a site for a town, which he called London, intending this to be his future capital, as he was not satisfied with the frontier position of Newark. Dorchester then interfered, and wished to secure this advantage for Kingston. As a sort of compromise the seat of government was ultimately fixed at York in 1796, (a few miles from where old Fort Toronto had stood.) In 1793, the further introduction of slaves was prohibited, and the term of existing contracts for servitude limited. The first Upper Canadian newspaper was about this time published at Newark. In the session of 1795 a bill was passed regulating the division between Upper and Lower Canada of duties paid on imported goods, whereby the former province was to receive one-eighth of the net amount. The first session of the second Parliament was hardly concluded at Newark when Simcoe was appointed governor of St. Domingo, and on his departure the government of Upper Canada devolved, for the time being, upon the Hon. P. Russell, President of the Council. By him the second session of the Parliament was held at York, which was at this time inhabited by twelve families. An act was passed making temporary provision for free intercourse with the United States in the way of trade and commerce, and in 1800 certain ports of entry were established. In the session of 1798 a bill was carried for determining the boundaries of the different townships. Next year President Russell was superseded by General Hunter, as Lieutenant-Governor of Upper Canada. The "Upper Canada Gazette" was begun at York about 1800. In 1803 the Talbot settlement was commenced in the Township of Dulwich on Lake Erie; where Colonel Talbot had received a grant of 5000 acres on condition that he placed one settler on every 200 acres. Various means had been taken by Parliament to promote the cultivation of hemp; seed was purchased and distributed, and in 1805 it was determined by law that £50 per ton should be paid for hemp. Governor Hunter died at Quebec on August 21st, 1805, where he was buried in the English Cathedral. Hon. A. Grant, President of the Council, administered affairs for a year until the appointment of Governor Francis Gore. During his rule an act was passed to establish public schools in every district of the Province, (1807.) The census of Upper Canada was first accurately taken in 1811, when the population amounted to 77,000.

LOWER CANADA, FROM 1792 TO 1812.

III.—In 1792, arrangements were made for having a monthly mail between Quebec and N. York, which, however, was not very regular as to time. In 1795, the harvest was so scanty that Lord Dorchester (Parliament not being in session) prohibited the exportation of grain from the Province. In July 1796, the Governor set out for home in the *Active* frigate, which was wrecked on Anticosti, but happily without loss of life. He continued his voyage from Halifax, and having reached England, General Prescott, whom he had left as administrator in Lower Canada, was appointed to succeed him as Governor, (1797.) At this time loud complaints began to be made respecting the fraudulent action of the Land-Granting Board, the members of which had appropriated large districts, to the prejudice of immigrants and other settlers. In 1799 Prescott was replaced by Sir Robt. Shore Milnes as Lieut.-Governor. Postal arrangements had been making great advances, and a weekly mail was now established between Montreal and the States. In 1803, Chief Justice Osgoode declared slavery inconsistent with the laws of the country, and all negroes held as slaves, over 300 in number, consequently received a grant of freedom. Land-jobbing was on the increase, and valuable grants were made to favourites and speculators, so that the general settlement and improvement of the country was greatly obstructed. An act was now introduced for the better regulation of pilots and shipping, and for the improvement of river-navigation from Montreal to the Gulf. This caused the establishment of the Trinity Houses, (1803.) In 1793, the first Protestant Bishop of Quebec, Dr. Jacob Mountain, had been appointed by the home government, who were anxious to build up a State-church in Canada; and about 1804 an Episcopal cathedral was erected at Quebec on the ruins of the Récollet church. Before leaving for England in 1805, Lieutenant-Governor Milnes had a difficulty with the House of Assembly, and arbitrarily prorogued it. President Dunn was left in charge of the government till the appointment of Sir James Craig in 1807. Some strictures on the conduct of Governor Milnes having appeared in the Montreal Gazette, the publisher of the paper was indicted for libel. The matter, however, was suffered to drop, whereupon the Quebec Mercury ridiculed the whole proceedings. The editor was forthwith arrested, and was released only upon condition of apologizing at the Bar of the House, (1806.)

IV.—About this time attempts were made, and chiefly owing to the representations of Bishop Mountain, to diffuse education. Directions were given by Parliament to establish free schools (which were to be maintained from the funds of the Jesuits, and where writing, arithmetic, and the English language were to be the chief branches of education) throughout the different Lower Canadian parishes, but the Roman Catholic clergy managed to frustrate this movement in great part, and grammar schools were opened only in Montreal and Quebec, (1806.) A French paper called "Le Canadien" appeared in November 1806, and began to decry the British population and the provincial Government, under the not-unfounded supposition that the *habitants* were looked upon as an inferior race. Apprehensions of a war with the United States were beginning to be felt, and therefore Sir James Craig, a distinguished officer who had served in the American war of 1774-7, was sent out to the colony as Governor-General. In November 1809, the first steamboat was seen on the St. Lawrence, plying between Montreal and Quebec. She was built by John Molson of the former city, and was named the *Accommodation*. The second Canadian steamboat, named the *Swiftsure*, was also built by Molson, and made her first passage from Montreal to Quebec (May 4, 1818) in the midst of the American war.

V.—Difficulties, which had been increasing in magnitude for several years past, reached a crisis in 1810. The Legislative Assembly wished to become independent of the other branches of the government; a majority of that body therefore required that all judges should be considered ineligible to hold a seat in the Lower House, inasmuch as they were influenced and removable by the Executive Council. This representative body, moreover, wished to exercise a general supervision over all Colonial affairs, and to gain this object the Assembly pledged itself to defray the whole expense of the civil administration. But Gov. Craig managed to parry these covert attacks upon his powers, whereupon the Assembly expelled Judge de Bonne, by a three-quarters vote. By way of rejoinder the Governor dissolved the House of Representatives, (1810.) This blow was followed by the forcible suppression of "Le Canadien," which had severely criticised the Executive, the seizure of its press, the imprisonment of its printer, as well as of three members of the Assembly and three other persons, who were never brought to trial. These despotic and unjustifiable measures caused this period to be designated "The Reign of Terror." The Governor was apparently seduced into these high-handed acts by the insinuations of his Council, who had acquired, and were anxious to maintain, an undue preponderance in the guidance of affairs. The Governor, in fact, was duped by his advisers, who represented the Canadians as factious and rebellious, and he only discovered his error when leaving the Province in 1811. The government was then administered by Mr. Dunn until the arrival of Sir Geo. Prevost, in September, as Governor-General of British North America. At the same time Major-General Sir Isaac Brock, the hero of Upper Canada, succeeded Lieutenant-Governor Francis Gore. War at this time was imminent between England and the States, and these two governors were selected with special reference to the critical position of colonial affairs, internally and externally. Sir George caused seven new members to be added to the Executive, (which caused satisfaction, inasmuch as the Executive body was well-nigh exclusively chosen from the Legislative Council, and hence of both bodies was the Assembly jealous,) and preferred to places of trust some of the members whom the former Governor had wronged. A militia bill was introduced, which authorized the Governor to embody two thousand unmarried men from eighteen to twenty-five years of age, for three months in the year, and in case of invasion, to retain them for twelve months. In June 1812, war was declared between England and the United

States, and the Canadians nobly cast aside any remaining dissatisfaction, and made the most zealous displays of loyalty and devotion to the British crown.

WAR OF 1812–15.

VI.—Prevost immediately notified American citizens living in Canada that they must leave the Province within fourteen days, and an embargo was laid upon all the shipping in the ports. With the consent of Parliament, army bills were issued bearing interest, as a substitute for money; and by this method specie was prevented from passing into the States. The regular forces in the colony amounted to only 4500 men, of whom no more than 1450 defended the Upper Province, though of more extended frontier and more exposed to attack than Eastern Canada. But the United Empire Loyalists rallied round the standard of General Brock, and in the Lower Province four battalions of militia were raised, and a regiment of Canadian Voltigeurs. Quebec was garrisoned by militia, and the regulars were moved to Montreal.

Canada was first invaded by General Hull on 12th July, who crossed the river at Detroit with 2500 men, and took possession of Sandwich. He issued a proclamation inviting the assistance of the colonists, and then proceeded to attack Amherstburg. But before he could effect anything of importance, Brock prorogued the Parliament at York, and arrived at the scene of action with about 300 regulars, 400 militia and 600 Indians. Hull's force had been somewhat reduced by sickness and other causes, and he consequently retreated across the river and shut himself up in Detroit. This place was forthwith invested by the Canadian army, and after a short resistance it capitulated, and Hull, and his entire army, were sent to Montreal as prisoners of war, (August 16.) Meanwhile another success had been gained in the West. Captain Roberts, stationed at St. Joseph's, an island in Lake Huron, under Brock's directions had captured the American Fort Michilimakinac (or Mackinac) without opposition, (July 17.)

VII.—The Americans now resolved to make a great effort upon the Niagara frontier. In September, more than 6000 troops were brought to the banks of the river, with a view of invading Canada. On October 13th Colonel Van Rensellaer sent over a detachment of 1000 men, who attacked the British position at Queenston. Rensellaer with a reinforcement then crossed in person, and his troops gained the heights. But at this moment, in the grey of the morning, General Brock, with an insufficient force of 600 men from the 49th regiment, advanced hastily from Fort George for the purpose of checking the enemy's advance. While cheering on his men to the attack, he fell mortally wounded and soon after died on the field. The 49th were discouraged and fell back, for the time, but in the afternoon a body of about 800 men, composed of regulars, militiamen and Chippewa Indians, under General Roger Sheaffe, (who succeeded to the civil and military command,) came to the rescue. After half-an-hour's fighting the Americans to the number of 900 surrendered at discretion. The British lost seventy men, while 400 killed and wounded was the loss which the enemy sustained. The Americans made another attempt to retrieve this campaign. General Smyth assembled 4500 men near Black Rock, in November, and crossed the river, but he was repulsed; and after some further untoward adventures, he decided that the expedition should be abandoned. Another success, however, awaited the British: Captain McDonnell crossed the St. Lawrence on the ice and attacked Ogdensburg, drove out the garrison and took some cannon and a quantity of stores.

VIII.—In January, 1813, the British Colonel Proctor defeated the Americans near Detroit and captured their leader, General Wilkinson, with 500 men. The enemy had meanwhile been equipping a naval armament at Sackett's Harbour, which gave them the command of Lake Ontario. A large force was also assembled under General Dearborn, and the plan of the oncoming campaign was limited to the conquest of Upper Canada, at this time defended by only 2100 men. In April the Republican General embarked about 2000 troops in Commodore Chauncey's fleet, and sailed to York. The capital was scarcely at all fortified, and was held by General Sheaffe with 600 men. The British were obliged to abandon the town, which was plundered and partly burned by the invaders. 200 militiamen surrendered themselves prisoners of war, and the artillery and naval stores were carried off. Sheaffe was censured for retreating, and before long he was superseded by Major General de Rottenburg. Dearborn and Chauncey now turned their whole available force upon Fort George at the entrance of the Niagara river. This post was gallantly defended by General Vincent with 1000 regulars and 300 militia, till the fortifications were dismantled by the enemy's cannonade, whereupon the British fell back upon Queenston, (May 1813.) Vincent then called in the garrisons of Chippewa and Fort Erie, and after destroying these posts, he retired to Burlington Heights. Upon this the Americans occupied all the Niagara frontier, and effected for the first time a lodgement in Canada.

Sir James Yeo having arrived from England with several officers of the Royal Navy and 450 seamen for the lakes, he and Governor Prevost hastened to Kingston to prepare the fleet for action. While the main body of the enemy was engaged at Niagara, an attack upon Sackett's Harbour was thought advisable, and about 1000 men were embarked on the British flotilla for this purpose. But the expedition shamefully miscarried, and Prevost's military reputation received a stain from which it never has become freed. Colonel Proctor's position at Detroit was again menaced by General Harrison, who wished to regain the Michigan territory. The American General had posted himself near the Miami rapids and was awaiting reinforcements. But Proctor did not wait to be attacked; he proceeded against the enemy with over 2000 regulars, militia, and Indians. His adversary, however, had found time to intrench himself, and Proctor's efforts were unavailing to dislodge him. The British, nevertheless, fell upon a reinforcement of 1200 men, which was advancing under General Clay, and made upwards of 500 prisoners. This loss crippled the Republicans, and secured Detroit from all immediate danger.

IX.—On the Niagara frontier, General Dearborn sent forward Generals Chandler and Winder to crush the British troops collected at Burlington Heights. But Colonel Harvey made a dexterous night-attack upon the enemy at Stony Creek, captured the two generals and 116 men, and caused the rest to retreat in great disorder. The British gained several other successes, chief among which was the surrender of Colonel Boerstler with 500 men, at Beaver Dams, to Lieutenant Fitzgibbon; so that the Americans held nothing on the right bank of the river except Fort George.

On Lake Champlain also the British arms were victorious. Two vessels of the enemy were taken at Isle aux Noix, and the magazines destroyed at Plattsburg and Swanton. But while this was going on, Commodore Chauncey was similarly employed on Lake Ontario in burning the barracks and stores at York. Our troops were now destined to experience some severe reverses, owing to the extraordinary exertions of the Americans. A squadron of nine sail under Commodore Perry attacked the British fleet on Lake Erie under Captain Barclay, and captured every vessel, (September 10.) In the same month, Harrison, having been joined by a fierce body of mounted riflemen from Kentucky, advanced towards Detroit in such force that General Proctor crossed the Detroit river and retreated up the Thames. On being followed by the Republican army of 3500 men, he made a stand at Moravian Town with 800 British, and 500 Indians under the brave Tecumseh. This noble Indian was killed, and Proctor retreated in confusion to Burlington Heights, in order to join the Niagara army. Harrison, flushed with triumph, marched to strengthen his countrymen in the same quarter.

X.—A grand plan of operations was now formed against Montreal. Two armies were to co-operate in this enterprise: the one of 6000 men under General Hampton from Lake Champlain; the other 8800 strong under Major-General Wilkinson, from Sackett's Harbour on Lake Ontario. Hampton found himself opposed at Chateauguay by a body of Canadians and Indians under De Salaberry and McDonnell, who manœuvred their small force of 400 so judiciously that the American General thought it prudent to retreat, and stationed himself for the winter at Plattsburg. Wilkinson's force now entered the St. Lawrence, and two detachments of 1000 each were landed at Williamsburg to disperse the Canadians who harassed their passage. The Americans under Boyd were attacked by a much inferior force under Morrison, and the (so-called) drawn battle of Chrystler's Farm was the result, (November 11.) But as the Republican force lost a general and over 200 killed and wounded, and were obliged to relinquish their position and re-embark in haste, it may be judged that our troops have the better claim to victory. Proceeding down the river, Wilkinson was notified of Hampton's retreat, whereupon he deemed it best to abandon his designs upon Montreal, and subsequently retired to Plattsburg.

Major-General McClure was now commanding on the Niagara frontier. On the advance of the British Colonel Murray, he crossed the river, after abandoning Fort George and reducing Newark to ashes. Murray gallantly followed him, surprised Fort Niagara, and took 400 prisoners. The British under Riall afterwards surprised and burned the frontier towns of Lewiston, Black Rock, Buffalo, and some others, by way of reprisal for the destruction of Newark; and so ended the campaign of 1813.

XI.—In the Assembly, which met in January, 1814, Chief Justice Sewell of Quebec was formally impeached, under seventeen heads of accusation, by Mr. J. Stuart, (afterwards himself Chief Justice.) Among the other charges were those of wrongly advising Governor Craig to dissolve the House, of sanctioning the arrest of three members, and the seizure of the opposition newspaper, and of sharing in the confederacy of John Henry. (This man had been sent out in 1809 by Sir J. Craig as a spy to ascertain the state of political feeling in the States; he conducted a secret correspondence with the Governor, which he afterwards disclosed to the United States Government for 50,000 dollars.) At the same time was presented another impeachment against Chief Justice Monk of Montreal, wherein he was charged with advising certain criminal prosecutions, and sitting in judgment upon them, and with having refused to grant a writ of Habeas Corpus. To rebut these accusations Sewell proceeded to England in June, and on his departure received complimentary addresses from the Executive and Legislative Councils. Aided by the influence of Prince Edward, he gained the good graces of Lord Bathurst, so that he and his colleague were exculpated, while he himself was highly recommended to Sir J. C. Sherbrooke, when this Governor arrived at Canada in 1816.

XII.—Warlike preparations had already recommenced in the spring of 1814. Colonel Williams with 1500 British had taken up his position at La Colle Mill, on the Richelieu, to protect Montreal, and here he was attacked in March by General Wilkinson with 4000 men. But the efforts of the Americans were vain, and they finally fell back again upon Plattsburg. In May the fort of Oswego was taken by the British General Drummond, where was found a quantity of ammunition and stores; but this success was almost balanced by the defeat at Sackett's Harbour which followed. Great attempts were again made upon the Niagara frontier by the Republicans. General Brown with 5000 Americans having crossed the river in July, took Fort Erie and its garrison of 170, and marching forward, he caused General Riall to retreat towards Burlington Heights. Brown then laid siege to Fort George, but finding it unexpectedly strong he retired to Chippewa. General Riall thereupon advanced, and the two armies met on the 25th July, and the battle of Lundy's Lane commenced. Fortune at first went against the British, and Riall was taken prisoner. But at this moment General Drummond arrived with a reinforcement of 800 men from York, and the Americans after six hours' hard fighting gave up the contest at midnight, and retreated in confusion to Fort Erie. The enemy in this fierce struggle numbered 5000 men, while our troops were under 3000. Drummond attempted to follow up his success by attacking Fort Erie, but he was twice repulsed with severe loss.

XIII.—After the abdication of Napoleon, England was enabled to turn more of her strength against the United States, but the results were very unsatisfactory. A strong force of 16,000 veteran troops was sent to Canada, and Sir George Prevost resolved to invade New York by way of Lake Champlain, where the British fleet might assist him. He marched to attack Plattsburg at the head of 11,000 men in September 1814. This place was now defended by General Macomb with no more than 1500 Americans and a few companies of militia. But the British flotilla having been destroyed by the enemy's naval force, Prevost conceived that even a successful attack upon Plattsburg would not be attended with any permanent advantage to him. Wherefore he gave orders to his army to withdraw, and in this humiliating manner terminated the most formidable expedition which had left the borders of Canada during the war. This luckless result afterwards exposed Prevost to a trial by court-martial, but he died before the charge against him could be investigated.

In Upper Canada General Brown sallied from Fort Erie in September with considerable loss to the British, and being afterwards joined by large reinforcements he obliged General Drummond to retire to Burlington Heights. The Americans gained farther advantages on Lake Erie, but they were repulsed in an attempt to recover Fort Mackinac. Drummond, being now strengthened by a detachment of the newly-arrived troops from Europe, advanced towards Fort Erie, in co-operation with Sir James Yeo at the head of the

British squadron on Lake Ontario. Brown thereupon, on November 5th, evacuated Fort Erie, after dismantling the works, and retired across the Niagara. Such was the last scene of this long and chequered Canadian drama of war, and peace was restored by the Treaty of Ghent, (December 24th, 1814,) whereby the contending parties were placed in exactly the same position they had occupied before the commencement of hostilities. In March 1815, the news reached Quebec, and peace was officially proclaimed by Governor Prevost. During this contest, the colonists, French and British alike, gave most effectual proofs of their loyalty to England, and it is universally acknowledged that the best safeguard of the Canadas was found, not in the external assistance afforded them, but in the bravery and vigilance of their own militia.

UPPER AND LOWER CANADA, FROM 1815 TO 1819.

XIV.—In 1815, a sum of £25,000 was granted for the purpose of opening a canal from Montreal to Lachine. In the Upper Canadian Parliament, £1700 was voted for the erection of a monument on Queenston Heights to the memory of the heroic Brock. In April, Prevost departed for England to clear his military reputation, and was succeeded by Sir George Gordon Drummond, (a native of Quebec,) as Administrator-in-Chief. Sir G. Drummond had previously held the government of Upper Canada, and was there replaced by the Hon. Francis Gore, as Lieutenant-Governor. The latter, being absent in England till September, was represented at first by Gen. Murray and then by Major-General Robinson. The U. C. Assembly, having begun in 1817 to consider the internal state of the province, was abruptly prorogued by the Governor. Robert Gourlay, a Scottish emigrant, indefatigable in exposing abuses, was at this time rising into notice, and soon became obnoxious to the government.

Next year the decision of the English Privy Council, discharging the accusations against Monk and Sewell, was announced to the Canadian Legislature, and the members of the Lower House resumed the consideration of the question. At this, Drummond, acting upon instructions from England, prorogued the Assembly of his own authority, a step which only increased popular irritation. This Governor was removed in May 1816, and Sir John Coape Sherbrooke, who had been Governor in Nova Scotia, was vested with the supreme command in British North America. This Governor saw at once and pointed out to the home authorities the fruitful source of Canadian dissensions, which arose from a want of confidence in the Executive Government. This sprung from the position which the Governor's advisers occupied in being irresponsible to the people, and in fact totally independent of them. A most fatal division, which time was only rendering more conspicuous, had now become manifest in the colonial government—namely, the systematic jealousies and opposition between the popular representative Assembly and the two Councils, Legislative and Executive. In 1816, common schools were established in Upper Canada, and £6000 was set apart for their use by Parliament.

XV.—In 1817, the first bank in Canada, that of Montreal, was opened in the city of the same name by an association of merchants—an example which was soon followed in the capital by the establishment of the Quebec Bank. In 1818, Lord Bathurst instructed his Excellency to accept of the offer formerly made by the Legislature to pay the whole civil list out of provincial funds. This being done, the control of the whole public expenditure became subject to the annual supervision of the House of Assembly. We now find the country divided into two parties, more distinct in their antagonism than had heretofore been apparent. The liberal party saw in this measure a salutary constitutional check upon the Executive Government; the Tory party regarded it as giving an undue power to the Assembly, and repudiated the principle of any one department of government being dependent for its efficiency upon an annual vote of supplies.

XVI.—A severe malady induced Sherbrooke to request his recall, and in July 1818 he was relieved by the Duke of Richmond. This nobleman was accompanied by his son-in-law, Sir Peregrine Maitland, who had been appointed Lieutenant-Governor of Upper Canada. After the peace of 1815 there commenced that steady tide of immigration into this country which has continued more or less to our own day. In the Lower Province these British immigrants found French laws and customs repugnant to their feelings, and they of course sided with their own countrymen, who formed the dominant party in Parliament. This movement aroused the alarm of the French, who dreaded less they should be totally swamped and deprived of all political existence; hence the Lower Canadian opposition was in the main composed of the French part of the population, many of whom, indeed, advocated the erection of a nationality independent of Great Britain. In the Upper Province a very diverse result was produced: there certain United Empire Loyalists, half-pay officers, and poor gentlemen, had formed themselves into a pseudo-aristocracy, and as such, frowned down all newcomers who might compete with them for political influence. The members of this exclusive party had managed, through course of time and general subserviency to the Governor, to monopolize all places of power and

trust under Government, and being woven together
by continual intermarriages they came to be styled the
Family Compact. In Upper Canada, therefore, the opposition gradually forming consisted not, as below, of
the old inhabitants, but of the recent settlers, who
justly considered themselves debarred from their right-
ful privileges.

UPPER CANADA, FROM 1819 TO 1829.

XVII.—When Maitland reached Upper Canada,
Gourlay was being prosecuted for libelling the government, which was filled with members of the
Family Compact. After two verdicts of acquittal, the
persecuted man was finally imprisoned, and he was
released, after long confinement had rendered him par-
tially insane, only to be banished from his adopted country. The Governor and Council, moreover, ordered at
this time the suppression of all public meetings. An
act was passed in 1820 nearly doubling the number of
representatives, and about the same time the Bank of
Upper Canada was established. Next year five new
Legislative Councillors were made, one of whom was
the Rev. John Strachan, afterwards the first Protestant
Bishop of Toronto. He soon rose to a prominent position among the Family Compact, and for many years
virtually directed the affairs of government. In 1824
the Welland Canal between Lakes Erie and Ontario
was begun, having been projected in 1818 by William
H. Merritt. Attempts were made by the Church of
Scotland to secure an appropriation of the Clergy Re-
serves, which the Episcopal Church had hitherto exclusively claimed; and in 1832 these efforts met with
success. The Canada Land Company was formed in
1824, which bought up immense tracts from the Crown

and Clergy Reserve Lands, at a trifling rate, and resold them in small lots at a large advance.

XVIII.—The Bidwell family had become an object of disfavour to the Compact, and attempts were made, but in vain, to prevent the return of young Mr. S. Bidwell, who finally rose to be Speaker of the House. The energetic W. L. Mackenzie also shared in this official dislike, and his paper, "The Colonial Advocate," was destroyed by a mob of *soi-disant* gentlemen at York, and the types thrown into the lake. In 1826 the Reformers had gained the upper hand in the Assembly, but many important bills were thrown out by the Upper House, which, as well as the Executive Council, contained Tory members only. A charter was now granted by George IV. for the establishment of King's College at York, and in 1828 it was endowed with large tracts of land formerly set apart for educational purposes. In 1828, Judge Willis, who took part with the people rather than with their oppressors, was dismissed from his situation on frivolous grounds by the Governor. Maitland, being shortly after appointed to the government of Nova Scotia, was succeeded by Sir John Colborne (afterwards Lord Seaton) in 1829.

LOWER CANADA FROM 1818 TO 1837.

XIX.—In Lower Canada, a serious difficulty arose between the Governor and the Assembly, during the incumbency of Richmond. He submitted the civil service estimates to Parliament, divided into branches, of which the total amount was given, but without any detailed statement of expenditure. The Lower House refused to sanction this, and voted that each payment should be in detail. This resolution was rejected by the Upper House, and the Duke had recourse to the irregular measure of drawing from the Receiver-General the sum required. In 1819, after a tour through the Province, the Governor was seized with an attack of hydrophobia, resulting from the bite of a tame fox, of which he died in August.

The government now devolved first on the Hon. James Monk, senior member of the Executive, and afterwards on Sir P. Maitland, who was superseded by the Earl of Dalhousie. This nobleman, promoted from Nova Scotia to the chief command of the British North American Provinces, arrived in June 1820. Dalhousie brought forward a scheme to obviate difficulties with the Assembly: he showed the members that the annual permanent revenue was not equal to the annual permanent public service money by a deficit of £22,000 sterling, and he therefore solicited this amount as a permanent grant. But the Lower House refused to grant anything beyond an annual bill of supply, in which every item was to be specified. The Legislative Council, however, again rejecting the supply bill, the Governor thought proper to draw the requisite money upon his own responsibility. In July 1821, the Lachine Canal was commenced by a Canadian company, previously incorporated for that purpose. During the summer the Governor visited the military posts of Upper Canada.

XX.—The lumber trade was becoming well developed; hundreds of ships were employed in exporting Canadian wood to Great Britain, and as a consequence of this demand, settlements took root on the Ottawa and elsewhere in remote regions, which, but for this branch of commerce, might have remained for years in their primeval desolateness. The Assembly had been making incessant efforts for many sessions to obtain the appointment of a Colonial agent at the English Court, but success had always been marred by the

8*

steady opposition of the Executive and Legislative Councils; this likewise occurred with several subsequent motions referring to the same subject.

In 1822 financial misunderstanding arose between the Canadas, respecting the proportion of import duties to which the Upper Province was entitled. The original eighth had been raised to a fifth, but even this was not deemed a fair allowance, on account of the rapid increase of Western population; and, moreover, arrears were claimed from Lower Canada to the extent of £30,000. The matter in dispute was referred to the arbitrament of the Imperial authorities, who, to settle all differences, proposed, among other things, a union of the two Provinces. This part of the bill was opposed by the English House of Commons, as trenching unnecessarily upon the rights of the colonists; the remainder, however, passed into law as the Canada Trade Act, which adjusted the difficulties, with judgment given in favour of the Western Province. Upon the contemplated union being mooted in the Provinces, almost unanimous objection was made to it in Lower Canada, both from Parliament and people.

The popular cause was strengthened in 1823, by the discovery that Sir John Caldwell, the Receiver-General, had become insolvent towards the Province in the sum of £96,000 sterling. About this time was settled, by commissioners appointed under the treaty of Ghent, the boundary-line between Canada and the United States, from St. Regis to the Lake of the Woods. In October, 1823, another official Gazette was commenced under Dalhousie's patronage, to the detriment of the old Quebec Gazette, now in the hands of Mr. Neilson, a powerful writer, who had always advocated the constitutional rights of the Canadians. This piece of ill-advised policy created many fresh enemies to the rule of the British Governor. In the next session the Assembly condemned the unlawful appropriation of public moneys, and reduced by one-fourth the amount demanded for the expenses of the civil administration. This House also put forward a claim to the administration of the whole public revenue, including such as was raised by the authority of the Imperial Parliament. Of all the members, Mr. Papineau in particular was loud in his denunciations of Governor Dalhousie's conduct, and proclaimed him as undeserving of public confidence. In 1824, the Governor founded at Quebec a Literary and Historical Society, which has effected not a little towards the elucidation of early Canadian history. In the same year an immense flatbottomed ship, named the *Columbus*, was launched at the island of Orleans, and sailed to England with a load of timber. Next year a still larger one, the *Baron Renfrew*, was launched at the same place, and after traversing the ocean was unfortunately wrecked off the French coast. These two vessels are the largest, except the *Vanderbilt* and the *Great Eastern*, that have ever crossed the Atlantic. Shortly after, Dalhousie sailed for England, leaving the charge of Lower Canada in the hands of the Lieutenant-Governor, Sir F. N. Burton.

XXI.—For four years affairs had been at a standstill; no progress had been made towards a satisfactory solution of the difficulties betwen the Assembly and the Crown. By the Lieutenant-Governor some of the points in dispute were conceded. A bill of supply was passed through both Houses, and sanctioned by the Governor, in which no distinction was made between the salaries of permanent and local officers. Previously the Government had insisted upon paying the Governor, the Lieutenant-Governor, and some other salaried functionaries, from certain revenues of which the Assembly desired to obtain the management. These revenues consisted of the produce of duties on imports, imposed by Act of the Imperial Parliament in 1774, yielding the annual sum of £35,000 sterling, with others of minor importance, arising from the sale of land, timber, &c. A parliamentary grant, therefore, having been made for governmental as well as popular expenditure, and this being accepted as legitimate, the proceeding amounted to a virtual acknowledgment of the Assembly's control over the whole revenue. The plan adopted by the House was to tender a round sum, in which was included the whole of the permanent Crown revenue and such part of the Provincial revenue as was sufficient to make up any deficiency of the former. The Home authorities disapproved of Burton's course, in compromising the permanent revenue, and on Dalhousie's return in 1826, a bill of supply was refused, in which the House similarly disposed of the entire revenue.

The University of McGill College at Montreal, founded and endowed by the Hon. James McGill, was now established by Royal Charter. In 1827, Dalhousie projected the erection of a monument to the memories of Wolfe and Montcalm; subscriptions were made, and the pillar now standing in Quebec was finished next year. In the session of 1827, Papineau was elected speaker of the Assembly by a large majority; this appointment the Governor refused to sanction, by reason of the persistent opposition which this member manifested towards the acts of the Administration. The House would choose no other Speaker, and the Governor accordingly prorogued the Parliament by proclamation. Acrimonious discussions now took place in the papers, which gave rise to many prosecutions for libel by the Government. In this year the Rideau

Canal, communicating between Kingston and the Ottawa, was commenced at the expense of the Imperial Treasury.

XXII.—In 1828, discontent had reached such a pitch, that 87,000 of the inhabitants petitioned the King, complaining of the conduct of successive Governors, including the Earl of Dalhousie, and urging a compliance with the claims of the Assembly. Viger, Neilson, and Cuvillier were deputed to present this petition. It was referred to a Committee of the British House, who recommended that the receipt and expenditure of the whole public revenue should be placed under the superintendence of the Canadian Assembly; but that, nevertheless, the Governor, the Judges, and the Executive Council, should be made independent of the annual votes of that body. The Committee most emphatically condemned the practice of appropriating large sums of provincial money without the consent of the representatives of the people, and advised that a more popular character should be given to the Legislative and Executive Councils. These suggestions gave great satisfaction to the Lower Canadians, and are known as "The Report of the Canada Committee of 1828."

Dalhousie was recalled and promoted to the military command of India, while Sir James Kempt was sent from Nova Scotia to redress grievances, and generally to carry out the recommendations of the Committee. Having called the Legislature together, he accepted the election of Papineau as Speaker, and by his liberal and conciliatory course gained the hearts of the people. Although an act transferring the disputed revenue into the hands of the Colonial Assembly, had not yet been passed, Kempt assured the House that it might be speedily expected from the Home Government.

New and popular members were added to the two Councils; and the Governor assented to a provisional Supply Bill similar to that for which Burton had been blamed. In 1829, the representation of Lower Canada was increased from fifty to eighty-four members. Next year Kempt returned to England, and was succeeded by Lord Aylmer. In Dec., 1830, the Colonial Minister, Lord Goderich, sent despatches, in which he informed the Governor as to the nature of his contemplated bill. Its chief feature was that the whole revenue was to be assigned to the Provincial Legislature, except certain sums which arose from the sale of land, the cutting of timber, and other casual sources. This despatch was laid before the Assembly, who forthwith passed a resolution "that under no circumstances, and upon no consideration whatever, would they abandon their claim to control over the whole public revenue." In 1831, "Le Canadien," which had been suppressed 21 years before, was re-established, and immediately commenced a warfare against Government. At this time there were about eighteen newspapers published in Upper Canada, among a population of 274,000; and in Lower Canada thirteen for a population of 898,000.—A proposal was made at Kingston to annex Montreal to the Upper Province, whereby a port of entry would be secured independently of Lower Canada; but the move was ineffectual.

XXIII.—In September, 1831, the Royal assent was given to a Bill introduced by Lord Howick, Under-Secretary of State for the Colonies, which transferred all funds—the casual and territorial revenue excepted—to the Colonial Assembly. The Jesuits' estates were likewise made over for educational purposes. Lord Aylmer was instructed to procure in return a grant of permanent salaries to the Judges, the Governor, and four of the chief Executive functionaries. In 1832, a disturbance took place at the Montreal elections, when the military were called out and fired into the mob, killing three and wounding two severely,—a circumstance which gave rise to extraordinary excitement. In the summer of this year the first Asiatic cholera broke out with fearful virulence, and spread in a very short time from Grosse Isle, the quarantine station, all over Canada.

The Assembly voted to the judges permanent salaries, which, however, were to be drawn first from the casual and territorial revenues. This was rejected by the Home authorities, who yet conceded the right to vote the Supply-bill by items. But the House refused to allow permanent provision to be made for the Governor and the four Executive officers, and this determination placed them completely at issue with the Crown. In 1833, difficulties again arose with Upper Canada, respecting the subdivision of duties, and in consequence the project was revived of uniting Montreal to the Western Province; this, however, was protested against by the Lower Canadian Parliament. In this year Montreal and Quebec were incorporated, and the first elections of Mayors took place. The Lower House now demanded that the existing Legislative Council should be abolished, and one substituted elected by the body of the people. Stanley, the Colonial Minister, opposed this, as inconsistent with monarchical institutions, and next year the Parliament in consequence declined to pass any Bill of Supplies, and prepared a long list of grievances, based upon the famous ninety-two resolutions. Meanwhile, £31,000 sterling was advanced from the military chest for the part-payment of the civil officers, whereby their responsibility to the Assembly was evaded.

XXIV.—In 1833, the French Canadian Press assumed a menacing tone; an organization took place at Montreal, where delegates sat under the style of "The Convention," and repudiated all interference of the British Government with the local affairs of Canada. A similar organization was also formed at Quebec, and named "The Constitutional Committee of Quebec." The Asiatic cholera again decimated the Upper and Lower Provinces during the summer of 1834. The last Parliament of Lower Canada met in February, 1835. Papineau was elected Speaker, and the members stated their wants in plain terms to Aylmer, especially insisting upon the Elective Legislative Council. They drew up a petition to the King, complaining of the headstrong conduct of the Governor, and of his preferring to office men from the minority, who were opposed to the popular cause, and also of executive usurpation, which could only be rectified by making the Council responsible to the people. The Lower House appointed John Arthur Roebuck, M. P., as their agent in England, where he was of no small service in explaining the difficulties which existed in the Canadian Government, and plainly warned the Home authorities that they would force the colonists into rebellion.

A commission of inquiry was sent out in August, 1835, composed of the Earl of Gosford, (who was also to relieve Aylmer as Governor,) Sir Charles Edward Grey, and Sir George Gipps. They were instructed to allow the Assembly's claim to the disposal of the entire revenue, on condition that provision for ten years was made for the Judges and Civil officers. An Elective Legislative Council was to be refused, as well as the surrendering of the management of the Crown Lands. Gosford convoked the Legislature the same year, in October, and his conduct towards the popular leaders was extremely conciliating, so that supplies were granted for the arrears of three years, as well as for six months in advance. Gosford is accused of duplicity, and of having led the Assembly, by hints of liberal instructions, to believe that all demands respecting the election of Legislative Councillors would be granted. The deception was soon discovered, and barred the way to all compromise. The Lower House refused the promised supplies; the Upper House, indignant at the attempts made to overthrow it, rejected almost every bill sent up from the Assembly, which Gosford soon prorogued. Every political element was thus disturbed, and violent collision was inevitable.

XXV.—In March, 1836, Mr. Speaker Papineau addressed a long letter to Mr. Bidwell, Speaker of the Upper Canadian House, in which was promised the co-operation of Lower Canada in all constitutional means to advance the best interests of their common country. Sir F. B. Head, at that time governing Upper Canada, referred to this letter when dissolving Parliament, and defied the interference of Lower Canadians. The English Commissioners now saw that things were at a stand-still, and believed it indispensable to obtain the money requisite for the working of government, without the Assembly's consent. They thought this would best be accomplished by the repeal of Lord Howick's bill, which had transferred £38,000 of revenue to the Assembly. The Colonial Minister, Lord Glenelg, was averse to this extreme measure, and instructed the Governor to make another effort with the Assembly. Parliament was accordingly assembled in September 1836; but the same position was firmly maintained, and the members resolved to adjourn their deliberations entirely, unless Government would begin the work of reform. The Commissioners had now returned to England with their report, in which a responsible Executive was recommended. But the Home Government resolved on decisive measures, and in March 1837, Lord John Russell moved a series of resolutions, which was carried by a majority of 269 to 46. It was resolved that £142,000 should be taken from the Provincial funds, and applied to the payment of judges and other civil functionaries; and that afterwards the government should be carried on, strict economy being observed, with the casual and territorial incomes. This step was in fact a suspension of the Canadian constitution. An elective Legislative Council and the responsibility of the Executive to the Assembly being declared inexpedient, amendments were promised in the formation of both. A small section of the House denounced the resolutions, and predicted civil war as the result of their enactment. By reason of the death of William IV. some delay occurred before action could be taken on Russell's motions, and in the interim, Gosford was notified to make a final appeal for supplies to the Canadian House.

XXVI.—Demonstrations against the Government had already taken place; meetings were held in which it was decided not again to apply for redress to the British Parliament, and a general convention was advocated as desirable. In June 1837, a system of organization was accordingly begun by Papineau, upon learning which Gosford applied to Sir Colin Campbell, (then Governor of Nova Scotia,) for a regiment, which reached Canada in July. In pursuance of Home instructions the Governor summoned the House together in August, and laid Russell's resolutions upon the table for consideration. By a majority of 46 to 31 these were branded as destructive to the representative government of the country, and the supplies were resolutely withheld. Lord Gosford with deep regret prorogued the House.

Recourse was now had to arms, that a separation might be effected from the mother country. A central committee was formed at Montreal, and Papineau took the supervision of everything. The Governor dismissed eighteen magistrates and thirty-five Militia officers, who took part in rebellious meetings. An association, called the "Sons of Liberty," paraded the streets of Montreal, in a hostile manner. In the County of Two Mountains, British authority was entirely disregarded, and an active training and arming was carried on among the malcontents. This example soon spread to the six Counties situate on the Richelieu and Yamaska, so that the Government applied to Sir C. Campbell for two other regiments, and also to Sir F. B. Head for some of his Upper Canadian troops,—while volunteer corps of loyal inhabitants were rapidly organized.

XXVII.—The first skirmish took place at Montreal, when the "Sons of Liberty" were put to flight, but without loss of life. The government now resolved to arrest the most active leaders, and warrants were issued against twenty-six, including Papineau. Nine were soon apprehended, but the master-spirit escaped. In the execution of these warrants, eighteen volunteers were sent to St. John on the Richelieu, but their return was intercepted at Longueuil by 300 armed rebels, who wounded some of the party and put the rest to flight. Papineau and other leaders were said to be at St. Denis and St. Charles on the Richelieu, and Sir John Colborne, Commander-in-Chief, sent detachments in November under Colonels Gore and Wetherall, to attack these villages. Gore met with such opposition at St. Denis, that his retreat was unavoidable, after he had lost six men killed and ten wounded. Wetherall, however, succeeded upon St. Charles, and drove out the rebels, who lost 300 of their number. In December, Gore, being reinforced, took possession of St. Denis without opposition, as a panic was beginning to spread among the *habitants*, and their leaders had already sought refuge in the neighbouring Republic.

A filibustering expedition of restless spirits from the States crossed the frontier, but it was frustrated by a party of British volunteers. And thus, in fourteen days, rebellion was quelled in the six Counties. Colborne afterwards turned his troops to the districts north of Montreal, where sedition had first arisen, and with slight opposition tranquillity was restored before the end of 1837.

UPPER CANADA FROM 1829 TO 1838.

XXVIII.—In Upper Canada, after the accession of Colborne to the Governorship, it was found that the casual and territorial revenues in the hands of the Crown had increased so much that the Executive was completely independent of the Assembly, so far as supplies for the civil list were concerned. The inhabitants of Toronto presented a petition to the Home Government, praying that the judges might not be subject to the control of the Executive, and that a local and responsible Government might be granted to the country. In 1829, Robert Baldwin appeared before the people as a candidate for Parliament, and Egerton Ryerson issued the prospectus of the *Christian Guardian*. In 1830, the Assembly asserted its right to control the whole Provincial Revenue, and, by way of retaliation, the Upper House threw out most of the bills presented to its consideration. In 1831, the Assembly made a permanent provision for the salaries of the Governor and certain other high officials, and received in return the entire management of the imperial, as well as all other, revenues. Thus was solved the difficulty which occasioned such profound agitation in Lower Canada. In 1832, Mackenzie was sent to England as the bearer of a petition from 24,500 colonists, who requested, among other things, that the Legislative Council should be made elective, the public revenue properly expended, and the land-granting department regulated. In 1834, an act was passed making the judges independent of the Crown. The Parliament of 1835 drew up the Seventh Grievance Report, which is chiefly devoted to the subject of Executive responsibility to the Assembly. The Executive now determined to secure the English Church in possession of a great portion of the Clergy-Reserves, (*i. e.*, a seventh part of the Provincial Territory which had been set apart by the Constitutional Act of 1791 for the support of Protestant Clergy,) and created fifty-seven Rectories, which were put into the hands of the ministry of the Episcopal Church. This intimate connection, it was thought, of land and owners would prevent the secularizing effects of any future legislation.

XXIX.—Colborne was superseded at his own request in 1835—(while at New York, on his return home, he received despatches constituting him Commander-in-Chief of the Canadian forces,)—by Sir Francis Bond Head, who received instructions much the same as those of Gosford. Of his own authority he began to appoint members of the Family Compact to lucrative offices which were vacant. He added also three highly popular members—Baldwin, Rolph, and Dunn—to the Executive; but, never consulting them upon any public measure, they shortly afterwards resigned. The Lower House took up the affair, and framed an address to the King, charging Head with " deviations from candour and truth." Difficulties increased until, for the first time, the supplies were stopped in 1836. The Governor now resolved upon a new election, and put forth such exertions that the Assembly became little more than a mere echo of his voice. The previous numbers of the Legislature had been forty Reformers and twenty Tories. After the elections of June, 1836, the Governor's influence changed these numbers into forty-one Tories and twenty Reformers; while, besides, the Reform and ultra-Reform leaders, Baldwin, Mackenzie, and Bidwell, were beaten at the polls. The new Parliament in 1837 introduced a bill erecting the first Court of Chancery in Upper Canada. Mackenzie, at the beginning of 1837, was holding meetings throughout the Home District, and keeping up a secret correspondence with the Lower Canadian malcontents.

XXX.—It was at this time that the troops were sent down to Lower Canada, and the Western Province was left unprotected. The withdrawal of the troops accelerated Mackenzie's movements, and he resolved to march upon the capital, with the intention of afterwards proclaiming a Republic. The rebels mustered on Yonge Street, (the great military road leading out of Toronto, which had been made under Governor Simcoe's directions,) and after an effectual attempt upon the city, they were routed at Montgomery's tavern by a militia force under Colonel MacNab and Justice McLean. Mackenzie, and most of the other leaders, fled to the States, while thousands of loyal volunteers, unapprised of the change of affairs, came flocking to the rescue of the capital, from all parts of the country.

In the London district there was an attempt at insurrection, but Colonel MacNab marched thither and dispersed all the rebels. The country had already become tranquil, when danger arose from another quarter. Mackenzie had collected at Buffalo a number of desperate characters, and with these he meditated an invasion of Canada. The command was assigned to Van Rensellaer, who took possession of Navy Island, in the Niagara channel, and fortified it. Volunteers were invited from Canada and the States, all manner of flattering promises being held forth, and soon the filibustering armament amounted to 1000 men. Colonel MacNab now arrived at Chippewa, and found himself at the head of 2,500 militia who were prepared to resist any attempt at landing. The steamboat *Caroline* was employed in the service of the (so-called) Patriots on Navy Island. MacNab gave orders for her capture; this was effected, and the boat, after being fired, was allowed to drift over the Falls. At this juncture, General Scott appeared on behalf of the American Government, to prevent any supplies or recruits from reaching Navy Island; where upon Van Rensellaer evacuated his position in January, 1838. Various bands of American adventurers were collected at Detroit, Sandusky, and Watertown, to invade Canada, but all efforts proved equally ineffectual.

XXXI.—In March, 1838, Sir F. B. Head was recalled, and Sir George Arthur appointed Governor in his stead. Five hundred political prisoners were at this time crowded within the gaols at Hamilton and Toronto. Two leaders—Lount and Matthews—were executed, others were sent to the Penitentiary at Kingston, while some were released. In May, Bill Johnson plundered and burned the steamer *Sir Robert Peel*, and escaped vengeance by taking refuge amidst the Thousand Islands. A few gangs of American "Sympathizers" crossed the frontier and effected some slight depredations. A final Patriot invasion was attempted, contemporaneously with the second Lower Canadian

Rebellion, in October, 1838. One body of invaders landed at Prescott, and ensconced themselves in a stone windmill. Here they were attacked by the Canadians, and after a lengthened struggle they surrendered at discretion. Further to the west, an assault was made at the same time upon Amherstburg, but the Sympathizers were defeated by Colonel Prince, and driven across the river to Detroit. Courts-martial were now formed—the chief prisoners were executed, while a large number (151 in all, including sixty-eight from Lower Canada) of the less conspicuous were transported to the penal settlements of New South Wales. These, and the exiled rebels generally, were allowed to return about five years after this, on account of the intercession of the Assembly on their behalf.

LOWER AND UPPER CANADA FROM 1838 TO THE UNION.

XXXII.—Returning to Lower Canada, we find that in June, 1838, Lord Gosford was recalled, and Sir John Colborne appointed Administrator of the Government. Martial law, which had prevailed from the outbreak of the rebellion, was discontinued in May; and in the same month arrived the Earl of Durham, in the double capacity of Governor-General and her Majesty's High Commissioner, to adjust all questions about civil government pending in Upper and Lower Canada. The Imperial Parliament also suspended the constitution of the country, and in its stead the Governor was empowered to form a Special Council, which should exercise the functions of both Houses. One of the first steps taken, was to hold in abeyance the Habeas Corpus Act, that the imprisoned rebels might be summarily dealt with. Every act of the new Governor was marked by liberality and disinterestedness. The Crown Lands Department was inquired into, and many abuses brought to light. By a bold expedient, which has been much criticised, the Governor disposed of all the political prisoners without the excitement of a formal trial : the minor offenders were pardoned, and eighty of the ringleaders were banished to the Bermudas. The British Parliament did not approve of his conduct, and passed an act of indemnity, setting aside Durham's Ordinance whereby the prisoners had been banished. On learning this, the Governor sent in his resignation, to the universal regret of the French and British populations alike. He advocated a Federal Union of the British North American Provinces, as a counterpoise to the extended territory of the States on the south. Before leaving his government, he made a tour through the Canadas, and prepared a Report so admirable in its accuracy and impartiality, that it holds an unsurpassed rank among official documents. It was owing to this report that the Union of the Canadas was resolved upon, Responsible Government introduced, and a general amelioration of Colonial policy effected. All lovers of our country must honour the Earl of Durham as the originator of good government in Canada. He left Quebec in November, 1838, and his place was filled by Sir J. Colborne, at first as Administrator, and then as Governor-General, (Jan. 1839.)

XXXIII.—Durham's departure seems to have been the signal for a second rebellious attack under Dr. Nelson. Martial law was again proclaimed in force, and the Habeas Corpus Act suspended. After sundry skirmishes, Sir John Colborne attacked Nelson at Napierville, and completely scattered his forces. The malcontents experienced another defeat at Beauharnois, from the Glengarry men; and with this the second Lower Canadian Rebellion ended, after a duration of seven days. Twelve rebels were then executed, and

Colborne followed up this stroke by suspending three judges, who, biassed in favour of the insurgents, pronounced his conduct unconstitutional. These functionaries were, after two years, reinstated by Lord Sydenham.

Several marauding incursions were made during winter by ruffian gangs from the States, who styled themselves *Hunters*, despite the vigilance and repressive measures of General Worth of the United States army. In June, 1839, Lord John Russell brought forward a Bill in the House of Commons, relating to the Union of the Canadas, that it might undergo discussion. Finnally it was laid over till next session, that more information might be acquired. Chief Justice Robinson, of Upper Canada, then in England, protested strongly against the projected Union; but in Upper Canada generally, it was popular. In October, (1839,) Mr. Charles Poulett Thompson, a British merchant, and President of the Board of Trade, arrived at Quebec as Governor General. Colborne, released from his arduous labours, immediately sailed for England, where he was honourably received, and elevated to the peerage as Lord Seaton.

XXXIV.—Meanwhile, Mr. Thompson convoked his Special Council, and explained the views of the British Ministry relative to the union of the Canadas, and the concession of Responsible Government, which was chiefly to be effected by rendering the principal members of the Executive dependent for their position upon the majority which their policy might secure in the House of Assembly. The Council immediately passed resolutions indicating their entire concurrence in the proposed action of the Home Government. The matter was thus settled, so far as concerned the Lower Canadian British population, and under the circumstances it was inexpedient to regard the opposition of the French, who were mostly disaffected.

The Governor then proceeded to Upper Canada, where more difficulty was experienced, inasmuch as the majority of the Upper House opposed the introduction of any liberal measure whatsoever. But the Governor published a circular despatch from Russell's pen, and by thus appealing to the loyalty of the Family Compact, he succeeded in getting the Union Bill introduced as a Government measure. It passed both Houses before the end of January, 1840, with stipulations that there should be an equal representation of each Province in the United Legislature,—that a sufficient permanent civil list should be granted, whereby the judicial bench might be rendered independent, and the indispensable business of Government prosecuted,—and that the public debt should be charged on the joint revenue of the United Province. The sanction of the Imperial Parliament was now the only thing required, and to expedite the receipt of this, the draft of a Union Bill was framed by Chief Justice Sir James Stuart. This was introduced by Russell, and with the exception of certain clauses relating to Municipalities, passed both Houses, and was sanctioned by the Queen on July 23d, 1840. Owing to a suspending clause, the bill did not come into operation until Feb 10, 1841, when, by proclamation, it was announced as law.

QUESTIONS TO CHAPTER II.

I. How many forms of government had Canada within thirty-two years? State what they were, with dates. What was about the population of the Canadas at the time of separation? What member of the royal family came to Canada in 1791? When did the first Parliament assemble in Upper and Lower Canada? State the number of members in each; where and by whom convened. What change was made in the names of the four upper Canadian districts? Give some other acts of this Parliament.

II. Where did Simcoe intend his future capital to be? Who interfered, and for what purpose? Where was it ultimately fixed, and when? What action was taken respecting slaves in 1793? Where was the first Upper Canadian paper published? How were the duties divided in 1795 between the Canadas? What change now took place in the government? When were ports of entry first established? Who was the next Governor of Upper Canada? What was the first paper published at York, and when? What action did the Parliament take respecting hemp? State the changes in government in 1805. When were public schools first established? When was the first accurate census of Upper Canada taken, and with what result?

III. What postal arrangement in 1792? Why and by whom was the exportation of grain prohibited in 1795? Who succeeded Dorchester? What operated to the prejudice of immigrants? When was slavery abolished in Lower Canada? What caused the establishment of the Trinity Houses? Who was the first Protestant Bishop of Quebec, and when appointed? When and where was an Episcopal Cathedral built? Who succeeded Milnes? How was the liberty of the press infringed upon?

IV. Who was instrumental in diffusing education in Lower Canada, and with what result? What French paper appeared in 1806? What course did it pursue? Why was Sir James Craig sent out? Give particulars respecting the first Canadian steamboat. Respecting the second.

V. When did internal difficulties reach a crisis? In what way did the Assembly seek to become independent? How did it seek to gain a control over all colonial affairs? What was the result? Of what despotic and unjustifiable measures was Governor Craig guilty? What was this period called? Why did the Governor so act? Who succeeded him? Who was now appointed to Lower Canada? What conciliatory measures did Prevost adopt? What militia bill was introduced? When was war declared?

VI. How did Prevost first act? How was specie prevented from passing into the States? What regulars were in the country, and how stationed? How were their small numbers reinforced? By whom, when, and where was Canada first invaded? Who hastened to attack him, and with what result? What success had Captain Roberts in the far west?

VII. Where did the Americans concentrate their efforts? Where did they open the attack? What success had Rensellaer? Who advanced to check him, and with what success? In what manner did the British ultimately succeed? What were their respective losses? How did the republicans seek to retrieve the campaign? How and by whom was Ogdensburg taken?

VIII. Describe Proctor's success near Detroit. Who had the command of Lake Ontario, and by what means? What was the plan of the campaign? Sketch the expedition against York. Where did the enemy next turn, and with what result? How did Vincent act? What was the position of the enemy? By whom was the British flotilla organized and manned? What was the result of Sackett's Harbour expedition? State the progress of events at Detroit.

IX. Describe the victory of the British at Stony Creek. What success was gained at Beaver-Dams? What did the Americans hold on the right bank of the Niagara? Which party was successful on Lake Champlain? How was this in part balanced? What victory did Perry's fleet gain? Describe Harrison's movements.

X. State the plan of operations formed against Montreal. How was Hampton checked? Sketch the movements of Wilkinson. Between whom, and with what result was the battle of Chrystler's farm fought? Describe the operations on the Niagara frontier.

XI. Who was impeached in 1814, and by whom? Mention some of the charges. Give some account of John Henry's mission. Who was also impeached, and on what grounds? What resulted from these impeachments?

XII. What operations took place on the Richelieu? What success and reverse did the British next experience? Detail the attempts made on the Niagara frontier. Sketch the battle of Lundy's Lane.

XIII. How was Prevost now strengthened? What did he resolve to do? What was the result? How were affairs in Upper Canada? How did the British regain Fort Erie? When was peace restored? What was the position of things after the treaty of peace? When was peace officially proclaimed at Quebec? What constituted the safety of Canada during this war?

XIV. What grants were made in 1815, and for what purposes? Why did Prevost depart, and who succeeded him? What changes took place in the administration of Upper Canada? Give an instance of Drummond's intolerance. What private man now became obnoxious to the government? Why did Drummond again prorogue the Assembly? Who succeeded him? What did this Governor see and point out? What fatal division now became evident? When were common schools established in Upper Canada?

XV. When and where was the first bank opened? Where was the next? What offer was accepted in 1818? What was the effect of this? How were the people now divided?

XVI. Why, when, and by whom was Sherbrooke relieved? Who was appointed to Upper Canada? What is noticeable after 1815? What was the result in Lower Canada? What in Upper Canada? What was the Family Compact?

XVII. Give a notice of Gourlay's persecution. What occurred in 1820? Who first came into notice next year? What canal was begun in 1824? Who projected it, and when? What attempts were made by the Scottish Church? When were they successful? Give a notice of the Canada Land Company.

XVIII. What person now fell into official dislike? When did the Reformers predominate in the Assembly, and what was the result? When and by whom was King's College endowed? How was Judge Willis treated? By whom was Maitland succeeded, and when?

XIX. What difficulty arose in Lower Canada? What was Richmond's fate? Upon whom did the government successively devolve? What scheme did Dalhousie bring forward? What was the result? What public work was commenced in 1821?

XX. What trade was increasing? What was the consequence? What efforts had the Assembly been making, and with what success? What misunderstanding arose in 1822? How was it adjusted? What project raised objection in the Canadas? How was the popular cause strengthened in 1823? What boundary was now settled? What newspaper change occurred in 1823? Detail what was going on in the Assembly. Who was conspicuous in his opposition? What society was founded in 1824, and what has it effected? Give some particulars as to the two great ships built near Quebec. Who governed in Dalhousie's absence?

XXI. What had been the position of affairs for four years? What concession was now made, and how? What revenues were claimed by the Crown? Show how the home authorities disapproved of Burton's conduct. What university was now established? What monument was erected in 1827? What fresh trouble arose with Parliament? When was the Rideau Canal commenced, and at whose expense?

XXII. Exemplify the discontent of 1828. Who presented the

petition? What did the British Parliamentary committee recommend? What did it condemn? What are these suggestions known as? To what post was Dalhousie appointed? Name his successor. How did he conciliate the Parliament and country? What assurance did he give the House? When was Lower Canadian representation increased, and to what extent? Who followed Kempt? What was the main feature of Goderich's bill? How did the Assembly receive it? What paper was re-established in 1831, and what was its course? Give the number of newspapers in Canada. What proposal was made at Kingston?

XXIII. What was now transferred to the Assembly? What was asked in return? Describe the first civil disturbance. How was the country afflicted in 1832? State the course pursued by the Assembly. What difficulty arose with Upper Canada? When were the first mayors elected in Canada, and where? What demand did the Lower House make? What arose from this? How were the civil officers partly paid?

XXIV. What was going on in 1833? When did the second cholera break forth? When did the last Lower Canadian Parliament meet? What was the tenor of the petition to the King? Who was appointed colonial agent? What action did England take in 1835? What instructions were given? How did Gosford succeed? Why were the supplies afterwards refused?

XXV. What celebrated letter passed between the two Parliaments in 1836? What did the commissioners propose? What was the effect of re-assembling Parliament? State the nature of Russell's resolutions. What delayed the execution of them?

XXVI. What was the state of affairs in Canada? Who commenced a system of organization? What did Gosford do? How did Parliament receive Russell's resolutions? How did the French Canadians act? Whom did Gosford dismiss? Where was British authority first disregarded? Where did the disaffection spread? How was the Government strengthened?

XXVII. Where was the first skirmish? What did the Government resolve upon, and with what result? What took place at St. John? What villages were attacked, and why? What success had Gore and Wetherall? From what quarter did assistance come to the rebels? Where did Colborne next turn his arms? When was peace restored?

XXVIII. How and in what respect did the Executive become independent in Upper Canada? What was the nature of the petition from Toronto? What notable men came forward in 1829? What claim did the Assembly make in 1830? How and when was one great difficulty settled? Who was sent to England with a petition, and what was its tenor? What act was passed in 1834? What was the chief Parliamentary action next year? What were the Clergy-Reserves, and when set apart? What did the Executive do respecting them in 1835?

XXIX. Who succeeded Colborne? To what office was Colborne appointed? How did Sir F. B. Head act respecting the Legislature? Why did the new Executive members resign? When were the supplies first stopped? What change took place in the complexion of the House? What bill did the new Parliament introduce? How was Mackenzie employed?

XXX. What accelerated Mackenzie's movements? Where and by whom were the rebels defeated? When was another attempt made at insurrection, and how quelled? What did Mackenzie next do? How did MacNab act? What caused the evacuation of Navy Island? What efforts were afterwards made, and with what success?

XXXI. When and by whom

was Head superseded? How were the prisoners treated? What outrage did Bi'l Johnson commit? When was the final Patriot invasion? Describe it. Where were the *Sympathizers* also defeated? What became of the imprisoned rebels?

XXXII. Who succeeded Gosford? What was the duration of martial law? In what capacities did Durham arrive? How did the Imperial Parliament act? What was the first step of the special council? How did Durham dispose of the prisoners? Why did Durham resign? What did He advocate? What is to be said of his report? What effect had it? Why is Durham to be honoured? Who succeeded him, and in what year?

XXXIII. What occurred after Durham's departure? Describe the second rebellion. How did Colborne act in this exigency? Who were the *Hunters?* What bill was brought forward, and by whom, in the British House in June, 1889? Who protested against this bill? Who was the next Governor? How was Colborne rewarded?

XXXIV. What was the new Governor's first step? What success did he meet with? What was his difficulty in Upper Canada, and how did he overcome it? What stipulations were attached to the bill and its passage? By whom was a draft of the Union bill framed? How was it received by the Home Government? When did it receive the Royal sanction? When did it come into operation?

CHAPTER III

FROM THE RE-UNION OF THE CANADAS TO THE PRESENT TIME.

I.—IN 1840, Queen's College, Kingston, was established, and Victoria College (founded eight years before) was incorporated as a University. After the Union, public attention was turned to the settlement of the Clergy-Reserves, which had long been a source of agitation. A Bill was brought forward in Upper Canada advocating their sale, and the partition of the proceeds, so that the largest share should fall to the Church of England. This was carried, but did not satisfy the Reformers, who still kept the question before the people. The germ of Responsible Government was now implanted in the Constitution, as may be seen from the words of the Governor's Message, "That he had been commanded by Her Majesty to administer the government in accordance with the well-understood wishes of the people; and to pay their feelings, as expressed through their representatives, the deference that was justly due to them." Towards the close of 1840, the imprisonment in the United States of Deputy Sheriff McLeod for his supposed share in the destruction of the *Caroline*, threatened to excite a general war. He was, however, acquitted and released, before any unpleasant consequences ensued.

Upon the formal re-union of the Provinces being proclaimed in February, 1841, a general election took place. Kingston was made the Seat of Government, where the Legislature was convened on June 13th—the Lieutenant-Governorship of Upper Canada came to an end, and Mr. Thompson, now raised to the peerage as Baron Sydenham of Kent and of Toronto, was entrusted with the sole authority. The Tory and Reform representatives from Western Canada were well-nigh equal in numbers, so that the French party held the balance of power—a position which it has occupied, more or less, ever since.

II.—Sydenham had many difficulties and prejudices to contend with, especially in the formation of the Legislative Council. But he triumphed over every obstacle, and introduced, through the Executive bills relating to the revision of Custom-house duties, the regulation of the currency, the extension of education, the formation of an efficient Board of Works, and the establishment of municipal corporations. Incessant exertion and anxiety had almost worn out his feeble constitution, when he was severely injured by a fall from his horse. This was sufficient to cause his death on the 19th Sept., 1841, and he was buried at Kingston in compliance with his own request. His name will be gratefully remembered, with that of Durham, whose policy he adopted, as one of the greatest benefactors of Canada.

Sydenham's successor, Sir Charles Bagot, a high-church Tory, arrived at the capital in January, 1842, and relieved Sir Richard Jackson, who, as commander of the forces, had been administering the Government. Baldwin and Hincks now came into power with the French party under Lafontaine, and, on accepting office, the Ministry went back to their constituents to be re-elected, in accordance with the principle of governmental responsibility to the people. Ill health induced Bagot to request his recall, (he died at Kingston in May, 1843,) and accordingly Sir Charles Metcalfe was appointed Governor-General of Canada, in the beginning of 1843. He manifested a decided leaning towards the Tory party, of which Sir A. MacNab (knighted for his services during the rebellion) was now a prominent member. This Governor maintained his right to appoint the Executive officers of the Crown, and on the resignation of the Ministry, he sought to form a Provisional Cabinet; but his conduct was denounced by the Reformers. In 1844, the seat of Government was removed to Montreal.

III.—A new election now took place, by which the Tories gained a small majority in the House, and their administration, under Mr. Draper, (Sir A. MacNab being Speaker,) lasted during the term of Metcalfe's, and his successor's governorship. In 1845, two large fires desolated Quebec and rendered 24,000 inhabitants houseless: Britain contributed £100,000 sterling to the relief of these unfortunates. Bad health compelled the Governor (who had been raised to the peerage as Baron Metcalfe, on account of his long and valuable services in India and elsewhere) to retire from his duties in November of this year, when Lieutenant-General Earl Cathcart, commander of the forces, was appointed Administrator. About this time the Ministry proposed to pay all losses caused by destruction of

10*

property during the rebellion in Upper Canada, by the sequestration of a special fund arising from tavern and other licenses. This was agreed to by the French party, provided that compensation should likewise be given for all losses sustained by the Loyalists in Lower Canada. Everything was thus satisfactorily arranged, and at the close of 1845, six Commissioners were appointed to classify carefully all just losses so sustained. But to obtain a correct and trustworthy classification seemed impossible—it was no easy matter to separate the innocent from the guilty—the rebels from the loyalists—and, as might be expected, the Commissioners (in April, 1846) presented a very unsatisfactory report, in which it was conjectured that £100,000 would suffice to pay all real losses. Mr. Draper's Ministry accordingly introduced a Bill ordering the issue of £9,986 in Provincial Debentures, to be applied to the partial payment of Lower Canadian Losses. In 1846, Common Schools were extensively established throughout the country, and the present educational system introduced, chiefly through the creditable exertions of Dr. Ryerson.

IV.—The Earl of Elgin, the new Governor of Canada, arrived at Montreal in January, 1847. The Tory Ministry was now in the last stages of decrepitude, and was being vigorously attacked by the Reform press under the guidance of the *Pilot*, a Montreal paper, edited by Mr. Hincks, (who had also established the Toronto *Examiner* in 1839.) Agitation was again becoming prevalent respecting the Clergy-Reserves' question, and their secularization was advocated by the Reformers. A Relief Fund was this year opened for the purpose of contributing to the wants of the famine-stricken poor of Scotland and Ireland. This famine now began to cause vast numbers of the destitute to emigrate to America, so that up to the beginning of August 70,000 emigrants had landed at Quebec. After the meeting of Parliament in June, Lord Elgin informed the Legislature that the British Government was ready to hand over to Canada the control of the Post Office department, and that the Canadian Houses were also empowered to repeal the differential duties in favour of British manufactures. Parliament was soon after dissolved, and Reform-Conventions were held all over the country in view of the new elections of January, 1848. The Reformers then proved completely triumphant at the polls, and nearly all their leaders were returned—Hincks, Baldwin, Price, Blake, and Malcolm Cameron. Dr. W. Nelson and Papineau were also sent from Lower Canada as representatives to the new Assembly. On the opening of Parliament, Mr. Draper's Ministry resigned, and the Baldwin-Lafontaine Government assumed the direction of affairs. Towards the close of the year, an important measure was passed in the repeal of the Imperial Navigation-Laws. This and the former repeal of differential duties insured to Canada the privileges of free trade. The colony was allowed to import goods whence and how she pleased; she was entrusted with the entire control of Provincial trade and the regulation of her own Tariff of Customs.

V.—Parliament was again convened in January, 1849, and the Governor remarked upon the completion of the St. Lawrence Canals which was brought about during the year, and the speedy transference of the Post Office Department to the Colonial Government. Mr. Lafontaine introduced a bill to pay the balance of Lower Canadian Rebellion-Losses, and a stormy debate followed. The Opposition contended that by its provisions actual rebels were to be remunerated, and that it was therefore doubly unfair for Upper Canada to pay any proportion whatsoever. The Ministry replied, that the object of the bill was only to pay for all destruction caused by the rebels, and to carry out the views of their predecessors in office in 1846, who had paid Upper Canadian losses from licenses forming part of the general consolidated fund, and had contemplated a similar provision, in part fulfilled for Lower Canadian Rebellion-Losses. But the Opposition members managed to spread their view of the question over the country, from Montreal westward, and monster meetings, denouncing Ministerial policy, were held, in which the common watchword was "No pay to Rebels." The antagonism of races broke forth again, and many members of the Ultra-Tory party threatened annexation to the States, sooner than submit to the consequences of Lafontaine's measures. Nevertheless the Bill was carried in the Assembly by 48 to 32, and having passed the Upper House, it was assented to by Lord Elgin, on April 26th, 1849. On leaving the Parliament House the Governor was insulted by the crowd, and in the evening a disorderly mob, to the lasting disgrace of Montreal, set fire to this building, which, with the valuable Library, (wherein were 1800 volumes on Canada alone,) was completely destroyed. Rioting was carried on in the city, and many Reform members were maltreated, and their houses injured. Similar scenes were enacted throughout Upper Canada, especially in Toronto, where Baldwin, and some others, were burnt in effigy. Some further attempts at violence taking place in the capital, the military fired into the mob, and one man was killed. Meanwhile, addresses, from the Reformers chiefly, came pouring in from all quarters to Lord Elgin, expressing their confidence in his Administration, and their regret for the scenes he had witnessed. The Governor nevertheless tendered his resignation, but all the Home authorities approved of his conduct, and requested him to continue in office. To this he consented, and the more gladly, inasmuch as the unfounded agitation was already beginning to subside.

In view of the late unseemly occurrences, it was resolved to remove the seat of Government from Montreal, and for the next two years to meet at Toronto, (its name had been changed from York in 1834.) Subsequent to this period the practice has continued of holding the sitting of both Houses for four years alternately in Quebec and Toronto, which, however, will shortly be done away with, by reason of the Queen's selection, in compliance with the wish of Parliament, of Ottawa (formerly Bytown), as the permanent seat of Government.

VI.—The repeal of the Corn Laws in England, in 1846, whereby all preference in favour of Canadian grain was abolished, and trade consequently diverted from the St. Lawrence, now began to produce telling effects upon the credit and revenue of the country, from which it took many years of industry and perseverance to recover. In 1849, a complete system of Municipal institutions was organized in Upper Canada, and in the following year a somewhat similar measure was introduced in Lower Canada. By this expedient, each district was entrusted with the management of its own local affairs, and the general revenue was relieved from any undue burdens which were more properly chargeable upon the localities benefitted. In 1850, the first proposition was made concerning Reciprocity, or free interchange of trade with the United States. In this year also the *Globe, Examiner*, and other Reform papers, commenced agitation afresh and persistently respecting the Clergy-Reserves' question, with a view to their secularization. A division thus arose in the Reform ranks, and the extreme party became known as Clear Grits. The free banking-system was now introduced, which provided for the issue of notes secured by the deposit of Provincial securities with the Receiver-General. In 1851, the Post Office Department was transferred to the control of the Canadian Government, and a uniform rate of letter-postage (3d. per ounce) was adopted. About this time railways began to be constructed, chiefly for the purpose of successful competition with the States for the immense carrying trade of the West. The first lines commenced were the Great Western, (projected by Sir A. MacNab,) the Northern, and the Grand Trunk. Numerous lighthouses had also by this time been erected in the St. Lawrence River and Gulf, to insure safety to navigation. Canada now made a very creditable display at the great industrial exhibition of the world's products held at London.

VII.—In October, 1851, Mr. Hincks became premier; he greatly forwarded the interests of the country, and especially identified himself with the prosecution of the Grand Trunk Railway. The Parliamentary session of 1852 is characterized as the Railroad Session, since, at this time, all existing railway-charters were amended, and many new ones granted. Montreal was this year desolated by a terrible fire, which deprived 10,000 people of their houses. In 1853, the elective franchise was reformed and extended, and the number of members in the Lower House augmented from 84 to 130.

The Reciprocity Treaty between Great Britain, Canada, and the other British North American Colonies of the one part, and the United States of the other, was finally concluded, after much negotiation, at Washington, in July, 1854, where Lord Elgin appeared as a special representative of the British Government. This was the first time that Great Britain recognized the right of the Colonies to participate in the framing of a treaty which concerned their interests. This treaty allows to Americans, with certain exceptions, the use of British sea-fisheries; it provides for a numerous list of commodities which may be interchanged free of duty, between the United States and the Colonies, and the third great feature is that it opens the navigation of the St. Lawrence and the Colonial Canals to Americans, while the right to navigate Lake Michigan is accorded to Canadians. In this year Lord Elgin was recalled, and was succeeded by Sir Edmund Head, the present Governor-General of British North America. In 1855, the Universal Exhibition was opened at Paris, and there Canada distinguished herself by carrying off one grand medal of honour, one medal of honour, thirteen first class and thirty second class medals, while forty-three of her contributors obtained honourable mention.

VIII.—A settlement of the Clergy-Reserves' question, satisfactory to the people, was now obtained. The Canadian Parliament, under the authority of an Imperial Act, separated the State entirely from all Church connection, commuted with the various incumbents, and after providing for the widows and orphans of the clergy, divided the remaining land and funds among Upper Canadian Municipalities. In Lower Canada, likewise, a great social change has recently been effected; the Feudal Tenure, which so long repressed the industrial efforts of its French population, has been abolished, with the consent of all parties interested. The rights of property have been respected by making an arrangement so that each tenant should pay a certain amount to his seigneur, while the requisite balance of about £650,000 should be made up by a contribution from united Canada. In 1856, the elective principle was introduced into the Legislative Council. The old nominees of the Crown are to retain their seats for life, but every new member is to be returned by one of forty-eight electoral divisions into which the Province has been mapped out for this special purpose. The Canadian Government has been obliged, in self-defence, to establish a weekly line of ocean steamships to England, at an annual expense of £45,000, in order to compete with the Cunard line, running to Boston and New York, which the Imperial Parliament had subsidized. Our line of ships has suffered greatly by the successive losses of the *Canadian, Indian,* and *Hungarian*; nevertheless, by the average of passages, it has been proved that the Canadian route is superior to any other, and a prosperous future may therefore be anticipated. In 1857, a severe commercial crisis passed over this country, which, combined with the bad harvest of that and the following years, depressed trade and business generally, to an alarming extent. In consequence of the falling off in the revenue, new customs acts were passed in 1858 and 1859, which imposed additional duties on many imported articles, and extended the *ad valorem* principle, in order to develope direct trade by sea between Canada and foreign countries. This policy seems to have met with success, and Canada is rapidly advancing to a higher and more influential position than she has ever yet occupied.

IX.—Attention began to be given about this time to the annexation of Red River settlement and certain portions of the territory adjoining, held by the Hudson's Bay Company, under a charter of Charles II., granted in 1670. Red River was first settled by fur-traders of the Company, but was not regularly colonized until after having been purchased in 1812 by Lord Selkirk, who established a number of industrious Scottish families in the wilderness. A few years after his death, the colony reverted into the hands of the Company, who repurchased it without the knowledge or consent of the inhabitants. The hardy Scottish settlers have survived all manner of vicissitudes: attacks of hostile Indians, violent opposition of the rival North-West Company, failure of crops, insufficient store-supplies, freshets of the river, ravages of insects, and of disease,—and form the nucleus of a flourishing settlement which now numbers 10,000 souls, including Christianized Indians and Canadian half-breeds.

The Hudson's Bay and North-West Companies were amalgamated in 1821, and a parliamentary license of exclusive trade in the vast regions between the Atlantic Ocean and the Rocky Mountains, north of Canada and the 49th parallel of North latitude, was granted to the united Company. This license was renewed in 1838, and the date of its expiration was 1859. A large proportion of the Canadians sought to prevent the renewal of this monopoly, questioned the validity of King Charles's charter, and agitated for the annexation of such portions of this region as would be available for colonization and for communication with British Columbia. To this movement the Imperial authorities seemed propitious; but owing, it is alleged, to the supineness and masterly inactivity of the Provincial Government, the scheme proved abortive, and it now seems the intention of Britain to erect the territory in question into a Crown Colony.

X.—In 1858, an act was passed providing for the protection and proper management of the Lake, Gulf, and River fisheries of this country; and in the same year were established reformatory prisons for juvenile offenders. The noble pile of buildings of the Provincial University at Toronto was now finished, and the Governor laid the cope-stone in October, with all customary ceremonies. The new Canadian Decimal Coinage came into circulation during this year. Victoria Bridge, the wonderful viaduct across the St. Lawrence at Montreal, has recently been completed, so that the Grand Trunk Line, comprising over 1000 miles of continuous road, forms one of the most comprehensive railway-systems in the world. In 1859, the Committee appointed some time previously to consolidate the statutory law of Canada, brought its labours to a successful completion, and the entire Canadian law is now within the reach of every one who can read.

As the Canadian people loyally extended their assistance to Britain in the shape of contributions to the Relief-Fund, towards the close of the Crimean war, so during the rebellion in India, a still more decided example was given of their devotion to the mother-country. An offer was made to raise a Canadian regiment, which should serve among the Imperial armies; this was accepted by the Home Government, and forthwith recruiting commenced in Toronto, Hamilton, London, Quebec, Montreal, and other places of lesser note, with such success, that in June, 1858, the Prince of Wales' Royal Canadian or Hundredth Regiment was embarked from our shores, *en route* for England. And we shall yet further have an opportunity of showing our loyalty in person to the young heir of England, whose anticipated arrival has already sent a preparatory stir from Gaspé to Sandwich; who, before these words pass into print, shall have come to show how highly our gracious

Sovereign values her Canadian subjects, and to learn with his own eyes how fair a jewel in Victoria's crown is our beautiful Canada.

QUESTIONS TO CHAPTER III.

I. What educational advancements mark 1840? What question attracted attention after the Union? What bill was carried? What was now implanted in the Constitution? What threatened to excite international war? Where was the Seat of Government fixed? In whom was the sole authority vested? What was the State of parties?

II. What difficulties did Sydenham encounter? What bills did he introduce? What caused his death, and when? Who was his successor? Who now came into power? What was done on their accepting office, and why? Why was Bagot superseded, and by whom? How did he disagree with his Ministry? What place succeeded Kingston as the capital, and when?

III. Of what complexion was the next Ministry, and how long did it administer affairs? State the circumstances of the fires of 1845. Why did Lord Metcalfe retire? What important measure was now brought forward? Describe the arrangement effected and subsequent proceedings. Give the chief event of 1846.

IV. Who was the next Governor-General? What was the state of the Tory Ministry? What papers did Mr. Hincks establish? What did the Reformers advocate? What Relief Fund was opened? How was emigration increased? and exemplify. Of what did Lord Elgin inform the House? What was the result of the next elections? Mention some Lower Canadian representatives. Who succeeded the Draper Ministry? What important action was taken by Parliament? What was the result for Canada?

V. What were the chief features in the Governor's speech of 1849? What bill was introduced? State the positions taken by the opposing parties. How was the country affected? By what numbers was the bill carried, and when sanctioned? What consequences ensued? How did the Reformers act? What was the Governor's resolution, and its result? How was Montreal punished? How is the alternating system to be abolished?

VI. What produced disastrous effects on Canada, and how? When were Municipal institutions organized, and for what purpose? What proposition was made in 1850? How were tho "Clear Grits" formed? Explain the free banking system, and when was it established? What departmental transference was made in 1851? What was the chief inducement to construct Railways? What lines were first commenced? How had navigation of the river been ensured?

VII. Who came into power in 1851, and what was the chief feature of his policy? What is the Session of 1852 called, and why? What political advances were made in 1853? When and between what parties was the Reciprocity Treaty concluded? What is remarkable about this Treaty? Define its chief articles. Who succeeded Lord Elgin? What success had Canada at the exhibition at Paris?

VIII. In what way was the Clergy-Reserves' question settled? What social change was effected in Lower Canada, and how? What recent change has been made in the Legislative Council? What gave rise to a Canadian line of steamers? What depressed trade in 1857 and 1858? What action did the Government take in consequence?

IX. What question assumed importance in 1857-'59? How was Red River first settled, and how afterwards colonized? What change occurred after Selkirk's death? Through what perils have the colonists survived? What is the population now? What Companies were amalgamated in 1821? What was granted to the united Company? What was the object of many Canadians in 1859? How did their scheme result?

X. State some remarkable events of 1858. What great undertaking was brought to a close in 1859? Give some recent instances of Canada's loyalty to Great Britain.

THE END.

www.ingramcontent.com/pod-product-compliance
Lightning Source LLC
Chambersburg PA
CBHW020123170426
43199CB00009B/616